The Essential Bu

LAND RO

DISCOVERY

Series II 1998-2004

Your marque expert:
James Taylor

Essential Buyer's Guide Series

Alfa Romeo Alfasud (Metcalfe)
Alfa Romeo Alfetta: all saloon/sedan models 1972 to 1984 & coupé models 1974 to 1987 (Metcalfe)
Alfa Romeo Giulia GT Coupé (Booker)
Alfa Romeo Giulia Spider (Booker)
Audi TT (Davies)
Audi TT Mk2 2006 to 2014 (Durnan)
Austin-Healey Big Healeys (Trummel)
BMW Boxer Twins (Henshaw)
BMW E30 3 Series 1981 to 1994 (Hosier)
BMW GS (Henshaw)
BMW X5 (Saunders)
BMW Z3 Roadster (Fishwick)
BMW Z4: E85 Roadster and E86 Coupe including M and Alpina 2003 to 2009 (Smitheram)
BSA 350, 441 & 500 Singles (Henshaw)
BSA 500 & 650 Twins (Henshaw)
BSA Bantam (Henshaw)
Choosing, Using & Maintaining Your Electric Bicycle (Henshaw)
Citroën 2CV (Paxton)
Citroën ID & DS (Heilig)
Cobra Replicas (Ayre)
Corvette C2 Sting Ray 1963-1967 (Falconer)
Datsun 240Z 1969 to 1973 (Newlyn)
DeLorean DMC-12 1981 to 1983 (Williams)
Ducati Bevel Twins (Falloon)
Ducati Desmodue Twins (Falloon)
Ducati Desmoquattro Twins – 851, 888, 916, 996, 998, ST4 1988 to 2004 (Falloon)
Fiat 500 & 600 (Bobbitt)
Ford Capri (Paxton)
Ford Escort Mk1 & Mk2 (Williamson)
Ford Model A – All Models 1927 to 1931 (Buckley)
Ford Model T – All models 1909 to 1927 (Barker)
Ford Mustang – First Generation 1964 to 1973 (Cook)
Ford Mustang (Cook)
Ford RS Cosworth Sierra & Escort (Williamson)
Harley-Davidson Big Twins (Henshaw)
Hillman Imp (Morgan)
Hinckley Triumph triples & fours 750, 900, 955, 1000, 1050, 1200 – 1991-2009 (Henshaw)
Honda CBR FireBlade (Henshaw)
Honda CBR600 Hurricane (Henshaw)
Honda SOHC Fours 1969-1984 (Henshaw)
Jaguar E-Type 3.8 & 4.2 litre (Crespin)
Jaguar E-type V12 5.3 litre (Crespin)
Jaguar Mark 1 & 2 (All models including Daimler 2.5-litre V8) 1955 to 1969 (Thorley)
Jaguar New XK 2005-2014 (Thorley)
Jaguar S-Type – 1999 to 2007 (Thorley)
Jaguar X-Type – 2001 to 2009 (Thorley)
Jaguar XJ-S (Crespin)
Jaguar XJ6, XJ8 & XJR (Thorley)
Jaguar XK 120, 140 & 150 (Thorley)
Jaguar XK8 & XKR (1996-2005) (Thorley)
Jaguar/Daimler XJ 1994-2003 (Crespin)
Jaguar/Daimler XJ40 (Crespin)
Jaguar/Daimler XJ6, XJ12 & Sovereign (Crespin)
Kawasaki Z1 & Z900 (Orritt)
Land Rover Discovery Series 1 (1989-1998) (Taylor)
Land Rover Discovery Series II (1998-2004) (Taylor)
Land Rover Series I, II & IIA (Thurman)
Land Rover Series III (Thurman)
Lotus Seven replicas & Caterham 7: 1973-2013 (Hawkins)
Mazda MX-5 Miata (Mk1 1989-97 & Mk2 98-2001) (Crook)
Mazda RX-8 (Parish)
Mercedes Benz Pagoda 230SL, 250SL & 280SL roadsters & coupés (Bass)
Mercedes-Benz 190: all 190 models (W201 series) 1982 to 1993 (Parish)
Mercedes-Benz 280-560SL & SLC (Bass)
Mercedes-Benz SL R129-series 1989 to 2001 (Parish)
Mercedes-Benz SLK (Bass)
Mercedes-Benz W123 (Parish)
Mercedes-Benz W124 – All models 1984-1997 (Zoporowski)
MG Midget & A-H Sprite (Horler)
MG TD, TF & TF1500 (Jones)
MGA 1955-1962 (Crosier)
MGB & MGB GT (Williams)
MGF & MG TF (Hawkins)
Mini (Paxton)
Morris Minor & 1000 (Newell)
Moto Guzzi 2-valve big twins (Falloon)
New Mini (Collins)
Norton Commando (Henshaw)
Peugeot 205 GTI (Blackburn)
Piaggio Scooters – all modern two-stroke & four-stroke automatic models 1991 to 2016 (Willis)
Porsche 911 (964) (Streather)
Porsche 911 (993) (Streather)
Porsche 911 (996) (Streather)
Porsche 911 (997) – Model years 2004 to 2009 (Streather)
Porsche 911 (997) – Second generation models 2009 to 2012 (Streather)
Porsche 911 Carrera 3.2 (Streather)
Porsche 911SC (Streather)
Porsche 924 – All models 1976 to 1988 (Hodgkins)
Porsche 928 (Hemmings)
Porsche 930 Turbo & 911 (930) Turbo (Streather)
Porsche 944 (Higgins)
Porsche 981 Boxster & Cayman (Streather)
Porsche 986 Boxster (Streather)
Porsche 987 Boxster and Cayman 1st generation (2005-2009) (Streather)
Porsche 987 Boxster and Cayman 2nd generation (2009-2012) (Streather)
Range Rover – First Generation models 1970 to 1996 (Taylor)
Rolls-Royce Silver Shadow & Bentley T-Series (Bobbitt)
Royal Enfield Bullet (Henshaw)
Subaru Impreza (Hobbs)
Sunbeam Alpine (Barker)
Triumph 350 & 500 Twins (Henshaw)
Triumph Bonneville (Henshaw)
Triumph Stag (Mort)
Triumph Thunderbird, Trophy & Tiger (Henshaw)
Triumph TR6 (Williams)
Triumph TR7 & TR8 (Williams)
Velocette 350 & 500 Singles 1946 to 1970 (Henshaw)
Vespa Scooters – Classic 2-stroke models 1960-2008 (Paxton)
Volkswagen Bus (Copping)
Volvo 700/900 Series (Beavis)
Volvo P1800/1800S, E & ES 1961 to 1973 (Murray)
VW Beetle (Copping)
VW Golf GTI (Copping)

www.veloce.co.uk

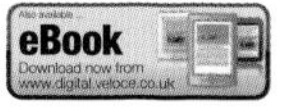

First published in August 2018 by Veloce Publishing Limited, Veloce House, Parkway Farm Business Park, Middle Farm Way, Poundbury, Dorchester, DT1 3AR, England. Tel +44 (0)1305 260068 / Fax 01305 250479 / e-mail info@veloce.co.uk / web www.veloce.co.uk or www.velocebooks.com.
ISBN: 978-1-787113-00-8 UPC: 6-36847-01300-4.
 British Library Cataloguing in Publication Data – A catalogue record for this book is available from the British Library. Typesetting, design and page make-up all by Veloce Publishing Ltd on Apple Mac. Printed in India by Replika Press.

Introduction

– the purpose of this book

This book is designed to help you buy a Series II Discovery that suits your needs and budget. It doesn't have to be in like-new condition, but it should be the best you can find within your budget, so that you get the best possible value for money. If you want to treat it as a pampered 'classic,' that's great. If you just want to enjoy owning and running one as an everyday vehicle, that's fine, too. One of the great things about the Series II Discovery is that it's a supremely practical everyday family vehicle. Oh, and let's not forget that it has quite astonishing off-road ability, in case you want to make use of that at the weekend.

The Series II was the second generation of Land Rover's Discovery range, the first generation of which had been so successful that the company was very cautious about changing it too much. However, when the Series II was new, Land Rover was owned by BMW, and because BMW was a stickler for quality control, the Series II Discovery was built to much higher standards than earlier Land Rovers. This shows in how well many of them have lasted.

I'll admit to being a complete fan of the Series II Discovery. I've had mine for 17 years, having bought it when it was just over a year old. I didn't expect to keep it this long, and I didn't expect to like it as much as I do. It's now

Most of the experience that has gone into this book comes from 17 years of owning this 2000-model Td5 ES.

V952 LOB has been a faithful family companion on many European holidays.

done well over 240,000 miles, and I hope it will carry on for a few thousand more. It's taken me and the family on several long trips across the European continent, and on camping expeditions with a four-person tent mounted on the roof. It's been my regular 'business' car as I keep to a fairly hectic journalistic schedule. Yes, it's beginning to need more maintenance than it did, and there are some quite serious jobs just over the horizon, but what on earth would I buy to replace it?

Land Rover built 279,019 Series II Discoverys in the six years from 1998 to 2004, and there are still plenty of them around in good condition. Many Land Rover enthusiasts recognise them as a classic of their kind, and it could well be that they eventually join the pantheon of classic cars in general. In the meantime, whether they do or they don't, I recommend that you find one, buy it, and enjoy it for what it is.

Thanks

I was lucky enough to be invited to the media launch of the Series II Discovery in 1998, and I was subsequently able to borrow a number of examples from the Land Rover press fleet for further evaluation. I've driven all kinds – including a 4.6-litre V8 while visiting the USA – and I'm grateful to all those who've made this experience possible. Special thanks, though, go to Stan Tooth at Turbo 4x4 in Reading, who looked after my own Series II for a dozen or more years and kept it in good health. Special thanks, too, to my wife Toni, who patiently understood the need for some of the more expensive repairs ...

Versatility: on a Spanish camp site, complete with four-person roof tent.

Longevity (fingers crossed): the distance recorder at the time of completing this book. Long may it continue.

Contents

The Essential Buyer's Guide™ currency
At the time of publication a BG unit of currency "●" equals approximately £1.00/US$1.33/Euro1.13. Please adjust to suit current exchange rates using Sterling as the base currency.

1 Is it the right car for you?

– marriage guidance

Tall and short drivers

There's plenty of headroom for tall drivers, and the wide seat adjustment range means that short drivers can get comfortable, too. However, it's quite a step up into a Discovery for short people, unless side steps are fitted.

Side steps can be a help for shorter people.

Controls

Many key switches are placed around the instrument binnacle, easily accessible, but others (down by the driver's knee) must be learned. Heating and ventilation controls are good, and with the automatic climate control system, they're excellent. Both manual and automatic gearboxes are good.

Will it fit in the garage?

A Series II Discovery is 185.2in (4705mm) long, and 86.2in (2190mm) wide over the door mirrors; with the mirrors folded, it's 74.4in (1890mm) wide. It's 76.4in (1940mm) tall without roof bars, but 77.9in (1980mm) tall with them fitted. You will probably have to fold the mirrors in for most domestic garages, and do check the height of the garage doorway carefully.

Several switches are positioned around the edge of the instrument panel. This is a top-specification ES model with leather upholstery.

Interior space

All Series II Discoverys will seat at least five people, but three adults on the rear seat will be uncomfortable on a long journey. The seven-seater models will certainly carry seven people, but the two rear seats are best for children.

Luggage capacity

The load area will carry enough luggage for

Some switches are less accessible, like these down by the driver's knee. That's a coin tray below them.

The standard heating and ventilation controls are easy to understand.

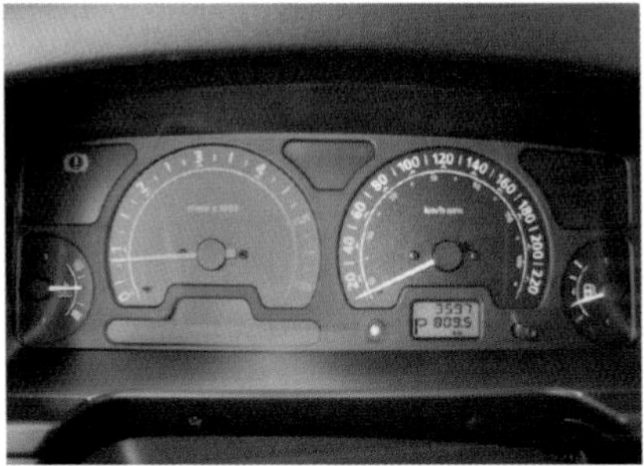

Instrument faces on the face-lift models from mid-2002 are fussier than the early type.

The 'curry hook' does exactly what its name suggests: it's for hanging the takeaway bag on when driving home.

Series II Discoverys come with five or seven seats. This is a top-model seven-seater.

four people on holiday. However, if the two rearmost seats in a seven-seater are occupied, there is no room for luggage. The second-row seats have a useful split-fold arrangement which makes the load area very versatile.

Usability

Good acceleration and cruising speeds, plus excellent braking and manoeuvrability, make a Series II Discovery perfectly acceptable for everyday use.

The rearmost seats in seven-seaters fold away into the sides of the body to leave a clear load space.

Parts availability

Most items to keep a Series II Discovery running are readily available. However, there have been shortages of less commonly needed parts (ignition locks and rear seat catches, for example), and there will probably be more in the future.

Plus points

The Series II Discovery is a versatile family vehicle that's great for towing and has excellent off-road ability. Most essential maintenance can be done on a DIY basis, although diagnostic equipment will be needed for many electronic items, such as the ABS.

Minus points

The ride quality is not as good as that of more recent 4x4 vehicles, and the fuel consumption of both diesel and petrol models is much higher.

2 Cost considerations

– affordable, or a money pit?

Servicing intervals

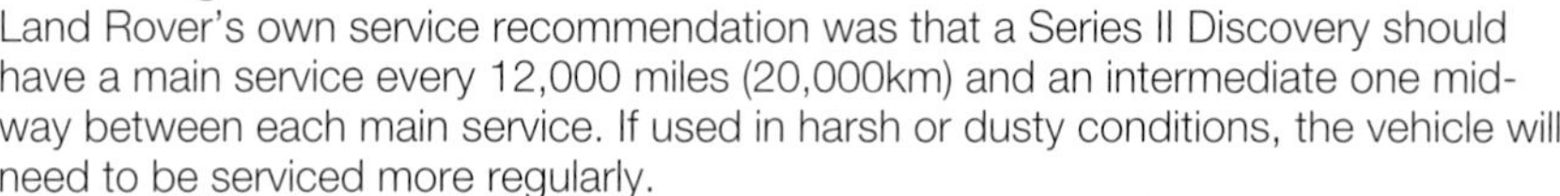

Land Rover's own service recommendation was that a Series II Discovery should have a main service every 12,000 miles (20,000km) and an intermediate one mid-way between each main service. If used in harsh or dusty conditions, the vehicle will need to be serviced more regularly.

A non-franchised specialist will typically charge around x500 for the main service, plus the cost of any additional parts needed, such as new brake pads, filters, and so on.

Sample parts prices

Please note that prices can vary considerably and that the cheapest is not always the best; nor is the most expensive! Many pattern parts are available, but not all are made to OE standards; the prices shown here are typical but you will find quite a wide variation. All prices are shown before tax is added.

Alternator: 120-amp type, for Td5	x160
Brake pads: front axle set	x20
Rear axle set	x15
Bumper finisher: rear corner	x40
Exhaust system: Td5	x450
V8, catalyst, aftermarket	x1150-2160
Headlamp: pre-face-lift	x40
Post-face-lift	x190 upwards
Radiator (depending on type)	x90 upwards
Rear air spring	x83
Shock absorber (depending on type)	x30
Steering damper	x20 upwards
Tyre (depending on type)	x90 upwards
Wiper blade: aftermarket	x5

Parts that are easy to find

Many mechanical items and all consumables – but in some cases you may have to compromise on quality. Aftermarket specialists have not yet invested much in remanufacturing structural items.

Parts that are hard to find

There are few items that are hard to find, although Land Rover does have periodic shortages of less commonly ordered parts.

Beware!

The Series II Discovery does have certain problem areas that can be expensive. See the chapters on evaluation.

3 Living with a Series II

– will you get along together?

There is an air of strength and dependability about the Series II Discovery, and the more you drive one, the more you come to trust it to get you where you're going, even in the most atrocious weather conditions. That is, as long as the vehicle has been properly maintained! Drivers particularly appreciate the Command Driving Position (inherited from the original Range Rover) that allows them to see over most other traffic and anticipate problems ahead. Meanwhile, the permanent four-wheel drive provides fuss-free traction and roadholding in the wet, plus the ability to press on through snow if necessary.

There is a high degree of comfort in a Series II Discovery. This is a late high-specification model – the last Series II ever built in fact

Still, this is no specialist off-road vehicle, despite its formidable abilities away from the tarmac. The Series II Discovery was designed to be a versatile and practical family estate car, and it's perfectly possible to own one of these vehicles for many years and never need (or want) to exploit its off-road capability. For many owners, the interior space and the feeling of safety that comes largely from the high seating position are enough justification for ownership. Plus, in many cases, the Discovery's highly regarded abilities as a towing vehicle for caravans or trailers, which are underpinned by the stability from its four-wheel drive.

As for running costs, a Td5 diesel Discovery is not a particularly expensive vehicle to drive, although the petrol V8s are to be avoided if you do high mileage. (Of course, an LPG conversion may make all the difference.) With a V8, you will struggle to do better than 18-20mpg on a regular basis, especially with an automatic gearbox, but the diesels should manage 25-30mpg. Personal experience with a diesel automatic that's been chipped is 27mpg in almost all conditions – less with the air-conditioning engaged.

Most Discoverys have cloth upholstery, as on this 2000 model.

Road performance is adequate, even 20 years after the Series II Discovery was introduced, and all variants accelerate

The Series II Discovery makes an excellent towing vehicle, and quickly became a caravanners' favourite.

surprisingly quickly when called upon to do so at normal motorway speeds. Although the lower-specification variants don't relish being hurled through corners, the better-equipped types with ACE anti-roll suspension and fatter tyres may surprise you with their ability – always tempered, of course, by the fact that these are tall and heavy vehicles subject to the laws of physics! The main area in which modern developments have overtaken the Series II Discovery is that of ride, where the heavy axles will thump about on uneven surfaces and can't equal the refinement of a modern independently-sprung vehicle.

Land Rover offered multiple options for adapting the vehicle to individual lifestyles, including folding tables. These are surprisingly rare.

You may have heard stories of Land Rover owners who do (or claim to do) absolutely no maintenance from one year to the next. Ignore them: a Discovery needs attention as frequently as an ordinary car, and its size and weight mean that lack of maintenance can soon lead to safety-related problems. As for who should look after it, there are many specialists who can do the job competently and affordably. However, not every village garage will be able – or even willing – to carry out the more complex jobs. A Discovery is not your average everyday saloon car, and sometimes needs specialist knowledge. There are many areas where it differs from the cars your local garage owner sees every day.

Many more enthusiastic Series II Discovery owners maintain their own vehicles. Routine servicing is not difficult, as long as you have a good workshop manual and the appropriate tools. A proper parts manual helps, too, and the ones produced by Land Rover contain exploded diagrams that are very useful for the DIY mechanic. Probably the best compromise is to do as much as possible of the routine maintenance yourself, but find a local specialist who will be able to help you

Another option was a double lid for the centre cubby box, providing concealed but readily accessible stowage for mobile phones.

The Series II is a very capable off-road vehicle as well.

out when you run into difficulties, or take on the more difficult jobs for you. Typically, the jobs that DIY maintenance can't cover are the ones that need specialist diagnostic equipment. Having said that, several affordable DIY-friendly diagnostic systems are becoming available.

Lastly, never forget the superb off-road ability that comes as standard with every Series II Discovery. Many enthusiasts buy them primarily so that they can take advantage of this. Some owners go for raised suspension and chunky tyres, but the truth is that such things are not necessary for most off-road use. A standard Series II Discovery has more than enough off-road ability for most situations – unless you are deliberately looking for challenges. Just remember that a towbar, if you have one, will hinder off-road performance because it will catch on the ground when driving up steep slopes, so take it off first.

Discoverys can be adapted, too. This is a second battery, fitted to power a fridge and other camping accessories.

4 Relative values
– which model for you?

The Series II Discovery range is fairly simple to understand. All models had five doors – there were no three-door types as with the earlier Discovery – and there was a choice of 4.0-litre petrol V8 and 2.5-litre turbocharged diesel (Td5) engines. Both engines were available with either a five-speed manual gearbox or a four-speed automatic.

All models had five doors (four plus the tail door). This is an early one, pictured during the 1998 media launch in Scotland.

By far the more popular engine in Europe was the Td5 diesel. There's not much to see of it under the bonnet.

Although multiple trim levels were offered during the six-year production run, the only major change came in autumn 2002. This was a face-lift, which brought different front and rear details (notably, overlapping, 'pocketed' headlamps), and interior revisions (like black instead of grey for the dashboard mouldings). These models didn't have the oval 'Series II' tail door badge that was used on the earlier types, because Land Rover wanted all the focus to be on the name 'Discovery' before the all-new Discovery 3 arrived in autumn 2004. In North America, where only petrol engines were ever available, these face-lifted Discoverys also had a larger 4.6-litre V8 engine.

So which should you buy? It's always best to buy on condition, but if there's a choice, you should go for the better-equipped models. They offer more features and won't cost significantly more than lower-specification types. As a guide, the trim levels began with S, went on through GS and XS

The V8 petrol engine is rather more visible when the bonnet is open. In fact, this is a 4.6-litre in a late US-model Discovery, but it looks the same as the 4.0-litre available elsewhere.

This 2001 GS model shows the style of alloy wheel that was current; it also has the body-colour front apron used on the more expensive variants.

Darkened 'privacy' glass was used to create a commercial or van variant. These have no rear seats!

The 2003 model-year face-lift brought a different front apron and 'pocketed' headlamps.

This badge on the tail door was used until mid-2002.

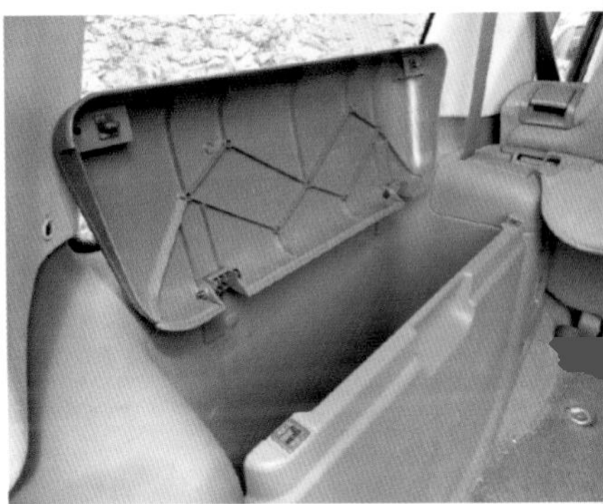
Five-seater models have these useful stowage bins in the rear, in place of the occasional seats.

(supposedly sporty), and the top model was the ES. From mid-2000 there was an even lower spec Discovery E, which remained rare, and the Adventurer replaced the XS. There were also several special editions, in each case with a combination of features not available elsewhere.

In Europe, the V8 models were rare, and the Td5 diesel is highly respected (though there were many doubting Thomases at the start who believed a five-cylinder engine must be the work of the devil!) In fact, it has gone on to become one of Land Rover's best-liked engines.

5 Before you view

– be well informed

To avoid a wasted journey, and the disappointment of finding that the Discovery doesn't match your expectations, it'll help if you're very clear about what questions you want to ask before you pick up the telephone. Some of these points might appear basic but when you're excited about the prospect of buying your dream classic, it's amazing how some of the most obvious things slip the mind ... Also check the current values of the model you're looking at in classic car magazines which give both a price guide and auction results.

Where is the car?

Is it going to be worth travelling to the next county/state, or even across a border? A locally advertised car, though it may not sound very interesting, can add to your knowledge for very little effort, so make a visit – it might even be better than expected.

Dealer or private sale

Establish early on if the car is being sold by its owner or a trader. A private owner should have all the history; don't be afraid to ask detailed questions. A dealer may have limited knowledge of a car's history, but should have some documentation. A dealer may offer a warranty/guarantee (ask for a printed copy) and finance.

Cost of collection and delivery

A dealer may be used to quoting for delivery by car transporter. A private owner may meet you halfway, but only agree to this after you have seen the car at the vendor's address to validate the documents. Conversely, you could meet halfway and agree the sale but insist on meeting at the vendor's address for the handover.

View – when and where

It's preferable to view at the vendor's home or business premises. With a private sale, the car's documentation should match the vendor's name and address. Arrange to view in daylight and avoid a wet day. Most cars look better in poor light or when wet.

Reason for sale

Do make it one of the first questions. Why is the car being sold and how long has it been with the current owner? How many previous owners?

Left-hand drive to right-hand drive

You are unlikely to find a steering conversion on a Discovery in the UK. If it has had one, it can only reduce the value and it may be that other aspects of the car still reflect the specification for a foreign market.

Condition (body/chassis/interior/mechanicals)

Ask for an honest appraisal of the car's condition. Ask specifically about some of the check items described in chapter 7.

All original specification

An original equipment car is invariably of higher value than a customised version.

Matching data/legal ownership

Do the VIN/chassis, engine numbers and licence plate match the official registration documents? Is the owner's name and address recorded in the official registration documents?

For those countries that require an annual test of roadworthiness, does the car have a document showing it complies (an MoT certificate in the UK, which can be verified on 0300 123 9000)?

If a smog/emissions certificate is mandatory, does the car have one?

If required, does the car carry a current road fund licence/licence plate tag?

Does the vendor own the car outright? Money might be owed to a finance company or bank: the car could even be stolen. Several organisations will supply the data on ownership, based on the car's licence plate number, for a fee. Such companies can often also tell you whether the car has been 'written-off' by an insurance company. In the UK these organisations can supply vehicle data:

DVSA	0300 123 9000
HPI	0845 300 8905
AA	0344 209 0754
DVLA	0844 306 9203
RAC	0330 159 0364

Other countries will have similar organisations.

Unleaded fuel

All petrol-engined Discoverys are capable of running on unleaded fuel without modification.

Insurance

Check with your existing insurer before setting out; your current policy might not cover you to drive the car if you do purchase it.

How you can pay

A cheque will take several days to clear and the seller may prefer to sell to a cash buyer. However, a banker's draft (a cheque issued by a bank) is as good as cash, but safer, so contact your own bank and become familiar with the formalities that are necessary to obtain one.

Buying at auction?

If the intention is to buy at auction, see chapter 10 for further advice.

Professional vehicle check (mechanical examination)

There are often marque/model specialists who will undertake professional examination of a vehicle on your behalf. Owners clubs will be able to put you in touch with such specialists.

Other organisations that will carry out a general professional check in the UK are:

AA	0800 056 8040 (motoring organisation with vehicle inspectors)
RAC	0330 159 0720 (motoring organisation with vehicle inspectors)

Other countries will have similar organisations.

6 Inspection equipment

– these items will really help

This book
Reading glasses (if you need them for close work)
Magnet (not powerful, a fridge magnet is ideal)
Torch
Probe (a small screwdriver works very well)
Overalls
Mirror on a stick
Digital camera
A friend, preferably a knowledgeable enthusiast

Before you rush out of the door, gather a few items that will help as you work your way around the Discovery. This book is designed to be your guide at every step, so take it along and use the check boxes to help you assess each area of the car you're interested in. Don't be afraid to let the seller see you using it.

Take your reading glasses if you need them to read documents and make close up inspections.

A magnet will help you check if the car is full of filler, or has fibreglass panels. Use the magnet to sample bodywork areas all around the car, but be careful not to damage the paintwork. Expect to find a little filler here and there, but not whole panels. There's nothing wrong with fibreglass panels, but a purist might want the Discovery to be as original as possible.

A torch with fresh batteries will be useful for peering into the wheelarches and under the vehicle.

A small screwdriver can be used – with care – as a probe, particularly in the wheelarches and on the underside. With this you should be able to check an area of severe corrosion, but be careful – if it's really bad the screwdriver might go right through the metal!

Be prepared to get dirty. Take along a pair of overalls, if you have them.

Fixing a mirror at an angle on the end of a stick may seem odd, but you may need it to help check the condition of the underside of the Discovery. It will also help you to peer into some of the important crevices. You can also use it, together with the torch, along the underside of the sills and on the floor.

If you have the use of a digital camera, take it along so that later you can study some areas of the car more closely. Take a picture of any part of the car that causes you concern, and seek a friend's opinion.

Ideally, have a friend or knowledgeable enthusiast accompany you: a second opinion is always valuable.

7 Fifteen minute evaluation
– walk away or stay?

Before you set off to look at a Series II Discovery for sale, make sure you know what variety to expect. It may have a Td5 engine, but is the gearbox manual or automatic? What is the trim and equipment level? You can find out more about what to expect from some of the books listed in chapter 16.

It is very easy to modify or upgrade a Discovery by adding non-original wheels, and some owners have even added face-lift-specification lights to early models to make them look newer. Such changes may not detract from the value of a vehicle, although they may make it valueless to somebody who wants one in original condition. On the other hand, such modifications may not bother you at all but rather make the vehicle closer to what you want. It's all personal preference.

You can often get a good idea of what to expect of the vehicle itself from the place where you go to look at it. Rough neighbourhood? Farmyard? Back-street dealer? Neat suburban drive? All these things can tell you things about a Discovery that the seller won't mention. Form your own opinion.

Exterior

It's only natural to have a good look round the outside of the vehicle as a first step. Stand back from it, too, and check that it sits square and doesn't lean to one side. You might be able to see scrapes and dents on the panels better from further away. What is the paintwork like? Is the glass in good condition, or are there chips and cracks in the windscreen? You can get a good indication of the overall condition of a Discovery by looking at the front and rear corners. Plenty of scrapes on the front spoiler or the rear bumper end caps are a sign of careless use.

Corrosion at the bottom of the tail door is a very common issue on the Series II Discovery.

What state are the wheels in? Alloys suffer from kerbing damage and corrosion. What about the tyres? Make sure they are radials of the correct size and speed rating; it is not unknown for sellers to put van tyres on because they are cheaper to buy.

Next, check the body panels

Minor damage can give a clue to how well the vehicle has been looked after. A cracked headlamp washer is often caused by minor supermarket car park knocks, for example.

Check for signs of kerbing damage on the wheels. This one seems to be in good condition, and still has the indented cap for its locking nut.

Warning lights are there for a reason: this one reveals a fault with the airbag system, which might prove expensive to put right.

for signs of corrosion. Series II Discoverys had galvanised lower panels and their bodywork doesn't normally rust, so any rusty panels might suggest poorly repaired accident damage. One major exception is at the bottom corners of the tail door, where the alloy outer skin is clenched over a steel frame. Corrosion causes the bottom of the steel inner frame to rust and the alloy outer skin will also be affected; the paint will bubble and lift in scabs, and the alloy will turn to a white powder. Repair is tricky – for which, read 'expensive.'

Under the bonnet

You should already know which engine to expect, so begin by taking a look under the bonnet to see what sort of condition it's in. Don't be surprised if the engine bay looks dusty, or even muddy. The Series II Discovery is a supremely competent off-road vehicle and may have been used off-road. Even if it's only been used once in wet and muddy conditions, mud will have been thrown up into the engine bay and stuck there. Very few owners go to the trouble of steam-cleaning the engine, and an engine bay that's slightly grubby will at least be honest.

A layer of dust will stick to the oil vapour that inevitably settles on all the components, and not many people bother to clean this off. However, if the whole engine bay seems to be oily, suspect problems such as oil leaks.

Check the oil level on the dipstick and check what colour that oil is. The blacker the oil, the longer it's been since it was last changed – you can compare your impression with what the seller tells you. Check the level of coolant in the header tank, which will give you a further idea of how well the vehicle has been looked after. A milky appearance to the coolant or a film of oil in the filler neck might point to head gasket trouble. On the Td5, look for smoky black marks above the exhaust manifold; this can warp, and the black

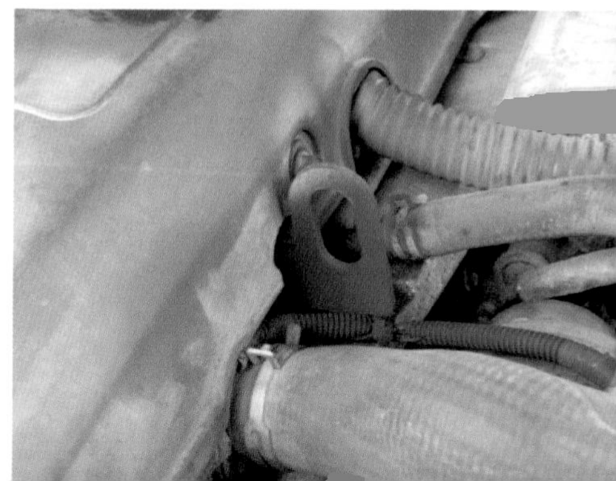

This black smoky mark on the engine indicates a leak where the exhaust manifold meets the cylinder head.

marks are made by exhaust leaking from the block-to-manifold joint.

How does the underbonnet wiring (to things such as the washer bottle or the level gauge on the header tank) look? Frayed wiring and corroded terminals mean trouble is lying in wait. On the V8 petrol engine, take a look at the ignition leads. Are they all clipped in their plastic guides, or are they loose and lying on the engine? With either engine, check the condition and tension of the auxiliary drivebelt. It should not be frayed, or loose, or too tight!

Start the engine, or ask the seller to do so. Does it start easily, or is there a lot of churning first? Diesels should start easily: the V8s sometimes hunt or stumble at first but should settle down quickly. Is there any smoke from the exhaust on start-up? How does the engine sound as it idles? With the bonnet open, any untoward noises that may be masked during a test drive may become much more apparent.

Underneath

First of all, have a look for any tell-tale signs on the ground below the vehicle. You are looking for oil stains (typically black), but also for leaks from the power steering and, where fitted, the ACE anti-roll suspension. The pipes for the ACE system can chafe and wear through, causing leaks; they're formidably expensive to replace.

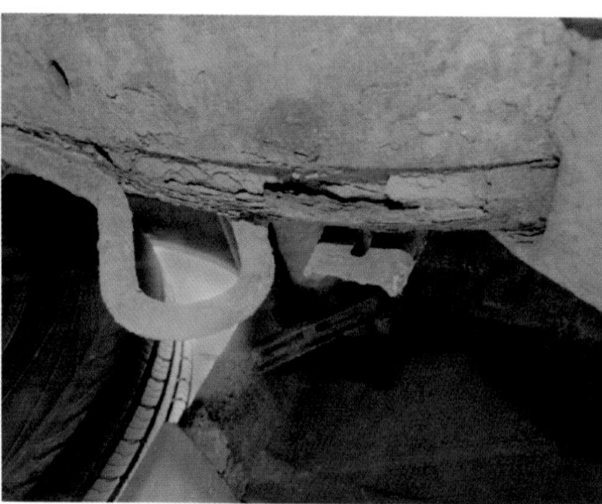

The rear chassis here is severely corroded and will not be cheap to repair.

Protect your clothes with overalls or a blanket on the ground, and crawl underneath. There's plenty of room because of the Discovery's high ground clearance. You're primarily looking for signs of corrosion on the chassis frame, and for indications of damage (typically to axle casings) that may have been sustained during off-road use.

The chassis frame is generally tough and rugged, but notoriously suffers from rust at the rear, each side of the fuel tank. What starts as slight corrosion will quickly develop into full-scale lamination and crustiness, which weakens the structure and will lead to refusal of a roadworthiness certificate (MoT in the UK). Major repairs in this area will be expensive, and a rusty rear chassis is one of the best reasons for not buying a vehicle. Be particularly suspicious of a rear chassis that has a thick coating of new-looking underseal. Tap the chassis with something like a coin if you're not sure: good metal gives a clear metallic ringing noise, but you'll hear a dull thud from corroded metal.

Look carefully for signs of welding. Weld repairs in themselves are not a bad thing – at least somebody has been looking after the vehicle – but cheap repairs are often done by welding sheet metal over a corroded section, and then plastering the whole area with thick underseal. It's better to see areas where the original black chassis paint has flaked off than to see the whole chassis caked in a thick compound that prevents you getting a good look at the metal underneath. If there's lots of underseal, have a feel around with a screwdriver to get an idea of what it's covering. If there's plenty of Waxoyl or a similar protective compound, at least one of the vehicle's owners has tried hard to keep it in good order.

On the inside

Leaking sunroofs have always been a major bugbear with the Series II Discovery, and for that reason good low-specification models aren't to be ignored: at least they don't have any sunroofs to leak!

Leaking sunroofs leave stains on the headlining, but with or without sunroof leaks, the headlining will suffer, eventually starting to part with its backing pad. A small amount of separation may be acceptable, but a seriously sagging headlining is not. Headlinings can be replaced, but are quite expensive and very time-consuming to fit. Don't imagine that you'll be able to repair the existing one with glue; you won't.

Have a good look at the condition of the front carpets, too. They can get wet if the front sunroof leaks, or if there's a fault in the sealing of the windscreen (which is bonded to the bodyshell). Water can eventually find its way under the carpets, where it will sit unnoticed on the steel floorpan. At the time of writing, rusted-out front floors weren't a major problem on the Series II Discovery, but it can only be a matter of time before they become one.

Take a look at the condition of the seats. If they are generally grubby, this suggests that the Discovery hasn't been very well looked after. Look especially for wear on the outboard edge of the driver's seat. Leather upholstery seems to last very well, often better than the fabric types. Worth knowing, too, is that it's

Top models have a useful compass embedded in the rear-view mirror. If it shows the letter C, it is not working – although it may correct itself.

Not all models have these pop-out cupholders in the rear armrest. Best to check them if they are fitted, because they can break.

The plastic stowage boxes on the tail door are vulnerable to damage from careless use.

Lower-spec models have this useful parcel shelf on the passenger's side. On the more expensive models, there is an airbag instead.

often simpler to replace a worn panel in a leather seat (or part-leather seat) than a similar one with all-fabric upholstery.

If the Discovery has air-conditioning, check that it blows cold air when engaged. If not, the problem may lie with the compressor (expensive) or with refrigerant pipes that have become holed through chafing (time-consuming to trace and replace.) With the automatic climate control system the air-conditioning is on by default. To turn it off you'll need to press the 'Econ' button. An Econ graphic will then appear on the control panel. Why Econ? That was a clever bit of marketing: Econ was for 'economy,' because the Discovery uses less fuel with the air-con switched off.

Most of the plastic trim items are strong and hard-wearing, so any damage may be an indication that this vehicle has had an unusually hard life. The most vulnerable is the oddments pocket inside the tail door, which often breaks after being carelessly closed against something hard in the load area.

Special editions

It's beyond the scope of this book to go into the minutiae of the special edition Discoverys. You'll need to take an expert along for that, or at least be very certain of what you expect to find before you go to a viewing. However, a couple of points are worth bearing in mind. One is that Land Rover often created special editions by adding accessories to otherwise basic models in order to boost sales at the bottom end of the Discovery range. Therefore, they aren't all laden with exotic options. Secondly, buyers generally assess special editions on their overall level of equipment rather than on their rarity; don't be tempted to pay over the odds.

There were multiple special editions over the years, but do you really want to pay extra for one?

How does it go/sound/feel?

The last element of this 15-minute initial evaluation is likely to be a short test drive. Don't forget that you'll need to be insured to drive the vehicle and not every insurance policy covers you for using somebody else's vehicle. Also worth checking is that the vehicle itself is road legal; if you take a test drive on a public road in a vehicle without a valid roadworthiness certificate, you will be breaking the law.

The Td5 engine has a distinctive and quite pleasing sound of its own, but listen carefully for a raspberry-like noise on acceleration, as this probably indicates trouble with the alignment of the exhaust manifold. Turbocharger boost should be undetectable as it cuts in, and there should be no sudden transition; check in the rear window for black smoke when accelerating, which could either be from wear in the injection system, or a turbocharger problem. In the unlikely event that the engine

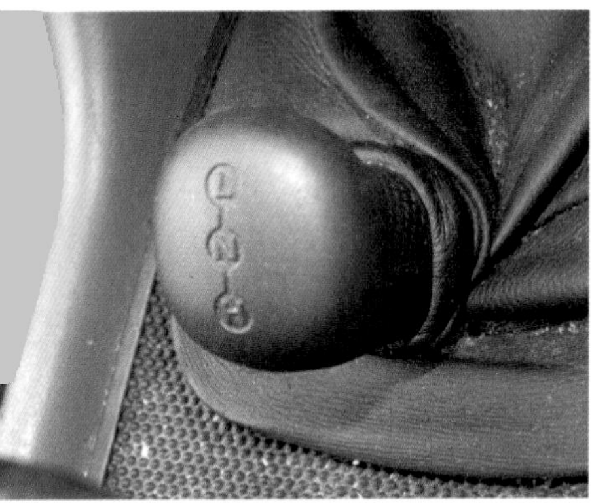

Check the operation of the transfer box lever. This is on an early model and is marked L-N-H (Low, Neutral, High), which means there is no manually-controllable centre differential lock.

The ABS warning light should come on as part of the automatic test cycle; if not, suspect a problem!

cuts out suddenly, suspect the well-known problem of engine oil seeping up the wiring loom for the injectors. This needs to be dealt with as quickly as possible before further damage occurs to the ECU, and is a very good reason for walking away from a potential Series II purchase.

Any V8 engine should always pull cleanly and smoothly, although high-mileage or neglected examples may have some top-end clatter from worn valve-gear. Keep an eye on the dashboard instruments for signs of overheating, which is always unwelcome in an all-aluminium engine.

Does the Discovery run in a straight line if you – very briefly – take your hands off the wheel? Does it pull up in a straight line when you brake? Incidentally, check that the ABS warning light on the instrument panel comes on when you turn the key and then goes out with the other lights as the check mode is completed; it's not unknown for an ABS fault to be disguised by removing the bulb from the warning light.

There should not be any driveline shunt; the Series II Discovery has a rubber coupling (called a 'doughnut') where the rear propshaft meets the differential to help damp it out. However, that rubber coupling can split after high mileages, and any metallic clunking in the driveline should be viewed with suspicion. You don't know how long the vehicle has been driven in that condition, or how much contingent wear or damage has been caused.

Some problems will be very obvious, such as the damage to the front corner on this late-model Series II Discovery.

With a manual gearbox, listen for gears that chatter on the over-run, and make sure that all gears can be selected, including reverse. Check that second and third don't jump out of engagement on the over-run. With the automatics, the changes should be smooth both up and down the gearbox, and if they aren't, there's a problem. Slurring on upchanges indicates wear.

Don't forget that the transfer box lever can seize up if unused for long periods. Select low ratio, and make sure it engages. Early Series II Discoverys didn't have a centre differential (although, bizarrely, the mechanism was present in the transfer box), instead relying on electronic traction control in difficult terrain. However, from mid-2002 there was a manually lockable centre differential to meet customer demand; if this is fitted, drive a short distance with the differential locked. Remember, though, that using diff lock on sealed surfaces can cause tyre wear. When you disengage the differential lock, you'll need to drive a few more yards before the warning light goes out.

Paperwork

Lastly, take a look at the paperwork. Is the seller's name on the documentation? Do the chassis and engine numbers match those on the vehicle? How long has the seller owned it? Problem vehicles are often sold on very quickly.

Only buy a vehicle from an individual who can prove that they are the person named in the vehicle's registration document (V5C in the UK) and, preferably, at the address shown in the document. Also check that the VIN or chassis number/frame and engine numbers of the car match the numbers in the registration document.

If the vehicle has been modified significantly, check that these modifications have the approval of the local authorities. In some countries, what you can do to a vehicle (for example, to improve its off-road ability) is limited by legislation.

8 Key points

– where to look for problems

After you've been for a preliminary look at the Discovery that's for sale, you'll want to spend some time thinking over what you've seen and deciding whether to go for a second look – which is what the next chapter is all about.

Thinking it over means sorting out the potentially confusing mass of information that you've just gathered so that you can make some sense of it. Begin by focussing on some fundamental questions:

- Is the vehicle structurally sound?
- Is it cosmetically acceptable?
- Does the engine seem good?

If the answers to all three of those questions are 'yes', you're probably going to want to go back for that second look. If you answer 'no' to any of them, you're probably going to be better off giving this one a miss.

Still tempted? All right then, here are a couple more deal-breaker questions:

- How much work will you have to do to it to make it meet your standards?
- Is it *really* the Discovery you want? For example, is it a five-seater when you really wanted a seven-seater?
- Are you going to have to do some tricky explaining to your wife/husband/ significant other when you get it home?

If you've been honest in your answers to these questions, and you still think you might buy the vehicle, move on to the next chapter.

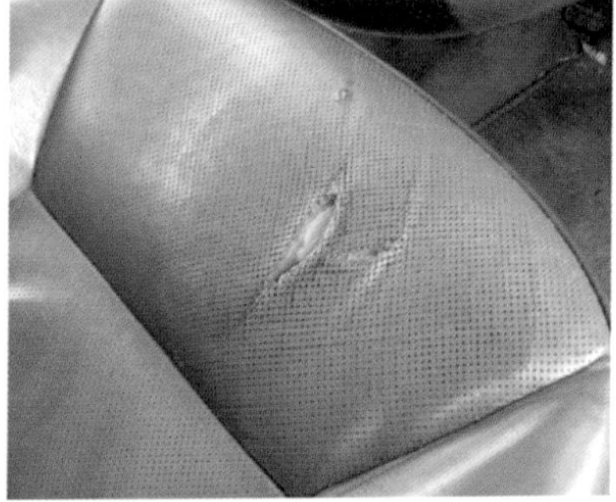

This kind of cosmetic damage may be acceptable, or you may want to get it repaired immediately.

Is it really the engine you wanted? A petrol V8 will cost much more to run than the Td5 diesel pictured here.

It would be a very understanding other half who thought you'd bought the right vehicle here: the air suspension has collapsed on the side nearer the camera and will need attention right away.

9 Serious evaluation

– 60 minutes for years of enjoyment

The best way to use this section is to tick the boxes as you go along, because you won't be able to remember all the details of the vehicle when you sit down to think about it later on. Score each section using the boxes as follows: 4 = Excellent; 3 = Good; 2 = Average; 1 = Poor. The evaluation procedure is explained at the end of the chapter. Be realistic in your marking!

The inspection sequence follows a logical order, so you'll start with the outside of the vehicle, move on to the interior, then examine the engine bay and the underside. Last of all, you'll take a test drive.

Paintwork 4 3 2 1

There were three types of paint available on Series II Discoverys. These were solid types (also known as c-o-b or clear-over-base types, with a clear protective varnish); metallic types; and micatallic types. Check for signs of touching-in and repainting, especially if the surface below feels uneven: the new paint may well be covering aluminium corrosion. It is not easy to get a good paint match for the metallic colours by doing a partial respray of a panel, and it will usually be very obvious if this has been done. Use it as a bargaining point if it has.

The paint finish on the Series II Discovery was generally very good when the vehicles were new, so be suspicious of areas where the paintwork seems to fall below standard. Typically, these will be areas that have been repainted, and it's a good idea to find out why the repainting had to be done. Was the vehicle involved in a collision? If so, this should alert you to look for other signs of damage that may be less visible. Expect to find a few stone chips on the leading edge of the bonnet and, as you'll have spotted in your preliminary evaluation, a few minor scrapes on the corners of the front apron spoiler.

Have a good look at the headlights on face-lift models, checking for damage; these are expensive to replace.

The 'eyebrows' on the wheelarches can sometimes develop a rough surface finish, as on the right-hand section here.

Body panels

The build quality of the Series II Discovery was much higher than it had previously been from Land Rover, so treat any signs of misaligned or poor-fitting panels with

Check the window frames where they enter the body of the door: this one has rusted and been repainted.

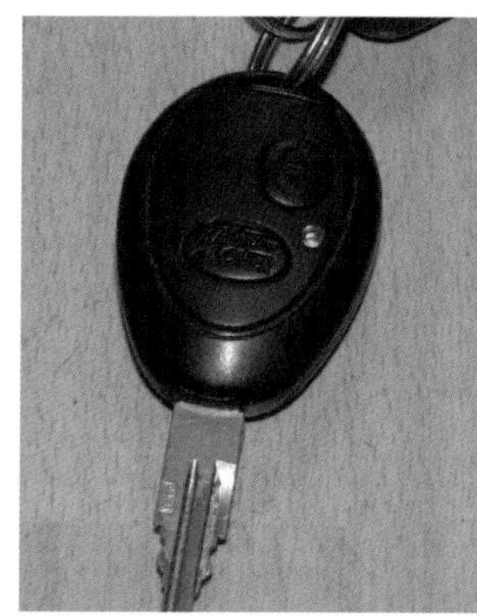

The central locking is operated remotely from the key grip. Make sure there are two sets of keys because these are expensive!

suspicion. It means that something has been replaced, and you'll need to find out why.

The good news is that the Series II Discovery rarely suffers from panel corrosion problems – except in the tail door, as explained later. If you do spot some, try to find out why it has occurred because it may indicate poor repairs after an accident.

Front wings/fenders

Check for signs of rust at the bottom rear edges of the front wings. The more expensive models, with wider tyres, have black plastic 'eyebrows' over the wheelarches. These shouldn't show signs of damage, although their surface can roughen over time so that they won't clean up well. It's not unknown for minor wing damage to occur if these 'eyebrows' get pushed inwards by contact with a gatepost or similar.

Bonnet

The bonnet panel on a Series II Discovery should be a first-class fit, and any uneven gaps between its edges and the front wings suggests accident damage and consequent panel replacement. The panel itself is alloy and unlikely to corrode, but stone chip damage can occur around the 'Land Rover' letters on the nose. If these chips have been touched in, the owner has tried to take care of the vehicle; if not, suspect the opposite.

A weakness of early models lay in the front door pillar, where the door stay can pull out. This one has been welded but has broken free again.

Doors   

4 3 2 1

The Series II Discovery's doors are panelled in steel, which was chosen to give better fit and finish than the alloy doors on earlier Land Rover models. They don't normally rust, but the window frames do. These are also made of steel and will rust just above the main door panel if the black surface coating is damaged.

Make sure the central locking locks and unlocks *all* the doors, because door lock problems are quite common. Sometimes, it's caused by nothing more than a spring, although replacement is a fiddly job and it's often wiser to replace the complete lock as a long-term measure.

Many early models were fitted with this strengthener, either by the factory or by dealers when the door stay problem became apparent.

Roof panel & sunroofs (if fitted)

4 3 2 1

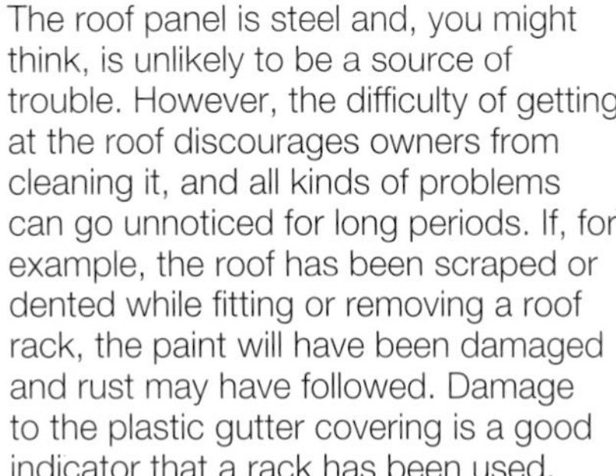

The roof panel is steel and, you might think, is unlikely to be a source of trouble. However, the difficulty of getting at the roof discourages owners from cleaning it, and all kinds of problems can go unnoticed for long periods. If, for example, the roof has been scraped or dented while fitting or removing a roof rack, the paint will have been damaged and rust may have followed. Damage to the plastic gutter covering is a good indicator that a rack has been used.

Check the roof bars for corrosion, and get up high to take a look at the roof panel itself.

Another problem can occur around the windscreen aperture, where the glass is bonded to the bodyshell. The factory-applied bonding was usually fine, but sometimes replacement windscreens aren't bonded in as well. Water gets behind the glass, sits against the metal lip, and sets up rusting in the roof panel.

There may be corrosion on the roof bars if the vehicle has them. They are made of aluminium alloy and will begin to corrode as soon as the black protective coating gets damaged and starts to flake off. Once again, use of a roof rack may have started this.

One of the biggest problems with the Series II Discovery is the sunroofs; there are either two or none. As a first check, make sure that the roofs (both manually-operated and electric types) actually open and that they close properly, too. Both types can seize through lack of use, and the motor of electric ones can burn out if the roof itself has seized. It's not unknown for owners to seal the roofs shut because they're plagued with leak problems. Borrow a chair or step-ladder to enable you to look closely at the sunroof frames. Traces of mastic around the edges are a sure indicator that a previous owner has had problems with leaks.

The main sources of sunroof leaks are the elbows to which the drain tubes connect. They are made of plastic and can fracture, so that the rainwater that should disappear down the tubes in the roof pillars is instead deposited on the inside of the headlining. It then leaks onto those sitting below. A sure sign of sunroof leak problems is stains on the headlining; look particularly in the area just above the windscreen and around the sunroof openings. Aftermarket replacements for the plastic elbows have been made available, and a new seal can often help, but sunroof leaks can be frustratingly elusive. Curing one set of leaks may well lead to another leak from somewhere else!

Some late models have these thicker roof bars, called 'Aero' bars, which were more for effect than real use.

Broken guttering like this is usually an indicator that a roof rack has been used.

Sills/rockers, side-steps 4 3 2 1

Tough plastic side sills run under the doors, and any signs of damage to these sills is worth investigating, because they're rarely damaged, even in off-road use.

A lot of Series II Discoverys were fitted with side steps (to help smaller people get into the tall vehicle), or with side runners, to protect the sills. Both are bolted to the chassis outriggers that support the body, and both are vulnerable to damage. It takes a pretty hard knock to bend such large and solid pieces of metal, so look for other damage that was caused at the same time. If a step or side

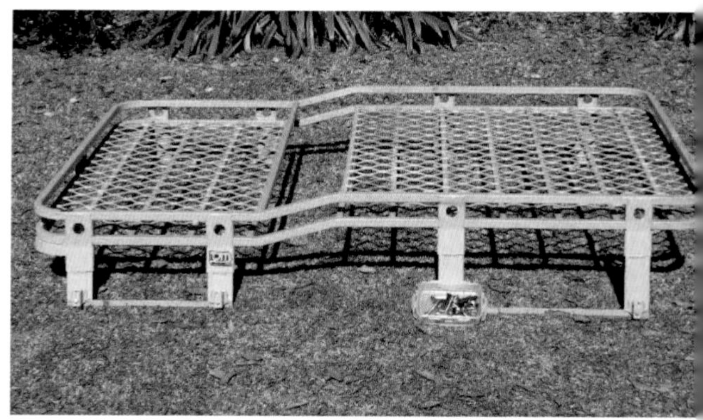

Gutter damage occurs when the rack is put on or taken off. Many racks are quite substantial, like this Australian-made example.

This is what happens to the windscreen frame if there is a gap in the bonding. The rust has spread up into the roof here.

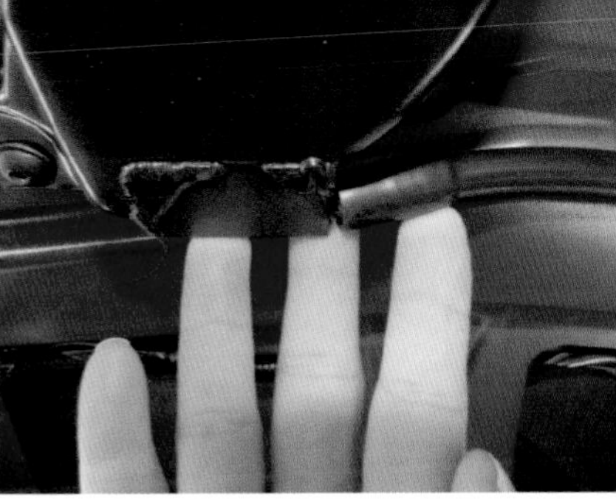

The 'elbows' of the sunroof drain are plastic and can fracture. The headlining has been taken down here.

runner is damaged on one side, remember that finding a matching replacement could be difficult, especially if the item is an aftermarket type rather than one manufactured by Land Rover.

Removing the headlining requires a lot of dismantling, and reveals just how much equipment it normally conceals.

Rear body sides   

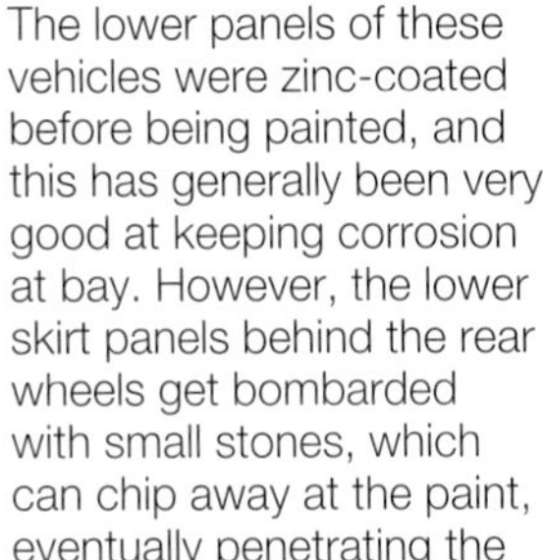

The lower panels of these vehicles were zinc-coated before being painted, and this has generally been very good at keeping corrosion at bay. However, the lower skirt panels behind the rear wheels get bombarded with small stones, which can chip away at the paint, eventually penetrating the zinc coating as well. Rusting will begin, but will probably be localised: the remaining zinc coating hinders its spread.

If these skirt panels are bent or otherwise damaged, the usual reason is that the vehicle has been used for some energetic (or careless) off-road driving.

Tail door   

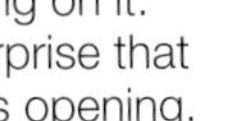

The tail door is big and heavy, made even more so by the spare wheel hung on it. Clutter in the pocket(s) on its inside face adds further weight, so it's no surprise that the door tends to drop on its hinges and drag against the lower edge of its opening. The hinges can also work loose, but it's easy enough to tighten their bolts.

You examined the Series II's favourite corrosion area in your preliminary evaluation when you looked at the lower corners of the rear door. Now take a

The rear bumper end should sit tightly against the bodywork. In this case, the lower body panel has been bent inwards during off-roading.

second, more careful, look. Once corrosion has set in here, it's hard to eradicate; it affects both the steel frame of the door and the outer aluminium alloy panel. Temporary cures are possible, although good ones are time-consuming and the only long-term answer is to fit a new door and to take good care of it. That will be very expensive, so a badly corroded tail door may be a good reason for walking away from a potential purchase.

Another potential problem area is the rear door lock, which may fail to operate with the rest of the central locking. The outer release handle may also stop working, even though the inner release works just fine. The cause is often a simple lock spring failure, which is easy enough to put right and not expensive, although access to do the job is tricky.

The engine bay

Unlike earlier Discoverys (and early Range Rovers), the front inner wings are not prone to rot through, so there should be no major problems in this area. The bulkhead is normally free from corrosion problems, too. As with other areas of the car that don't usually give trouble, any signs of corrosion in either area will probably be the result of poorly repaired accident damage.

Before looking at the engine itself, take a moment to check fluid levels. Oil is easily checked with the dipstick; coolant is easily checked by a look at the transparent header tank. Also transparent (although often caked with dirt) are the reservoirs for the power steering fluid and the ACE suspension fluid, which are combined into a single unit with two compartments when both systems are fitted, so are also easy to check.

Few Series II Discoverys won't have their original or original-type engine, because both the petrol V8 and the Td5 diesel were well-liked and reliable. However, it's quite common to find that either

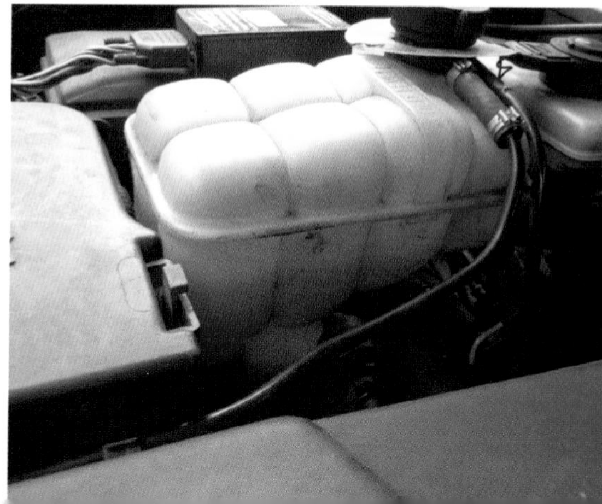

Check the level of coolant in the header tank. It should be up to the ridge running around the outside. Make sure the recommended type of coolant (OAT) has been used, too.

engine has been tuned for greater power, typically by means of a replacement or 'piggy-back' ECU chip. Several aftermarket specialists offered these, and a chip-tuned engine should not normally be a cause for concern. The author's experience of a Td5 chip-tuned to 173bhp (from the standard 136bhp) over some 170,000 miles has been entirely positive.

Don't be afraid of good-quality aftermarket tuning chips. This 'piggy-back' type has served the author's Td5 Discovery well for around 170,000 miles.

However, remember that the automatic gearbox is protected by a torque limiter. If the input torque from the engine exceeds a set amount, this will cause the engine ECU to go into 'limp home' mode. (It will then reset itself when the ignition is turned off.) The manual gearbox is not protected in the same way, and chips designed for use with this typically allow the engine to deliver more torque. It's therefore theoretically possible to install a chip intended for a Td5 with a manual gearbox into one with an automatic gearbox, with predictable results. If the Discovery you're looking at seems prone to switching to 'limp home' mode (which will be apparent during the test drive you'll take later), this could be a cause. Note that less restrictive 'sports' exhaust systems combined with the correct chip for an automatic Td5 might cause the same problem.

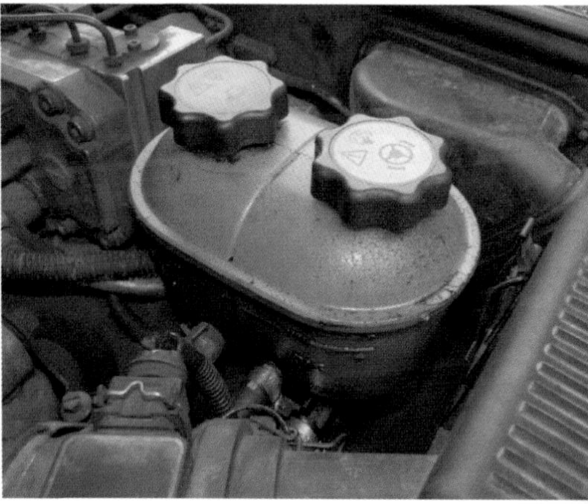
Something else to check: this is the twin reservoir for PAS and ACE fluid.

During your preliminary evaluation, you formed an opinion of how well the engine has been maintained. The next thing is to listen to it running.

The Td5 diesel is not a particularly noisy engine, although it is a lot noisier than most modern diesels. Listen for odd noises, especially the 'raspberry' from a warped exhaust manifold; as explained during the preliminary evaluation, there are likely to be visible signs of this problem as well, but the seller might have wiped the engine clean. For reassurance, the Td5 diesel has a chain-driven camshaft and therefore does not need regular cambelt changes like the earlier Tdi diesel engines. The timing chain also has a tensioner which should remove most of the slack as the chain wears with age; for this reason, a noisy timing chain is something to avoid.

The petrol V8 is much quieter and smoother. If there's a lot of top-end noise, there's probably wear in the hydraulic tappets and maybe the camshaft as well. In anything other than a high-mileage engine this means that oil changes have been neglected. If an LPG conversion has been fitted, there will be a fuel changeover unit that allows the engine to be run on either petrol or LPG.

Generally, the quieter and smoother a V8 engine sounds, the better condition it's likely to be in. These engines need clean oil every 6000 miles, so for peace of mind, ask the owner when the oil was last changed, and confirm that yourself by checking its colour on the dipstick. Black oil indicates an oil change is overdue, and signs of thick black sludge around the oil filler cap mean that maintenance has been neglected in the longer term.

Checking under the car

During your preliminary evaluation, you took a look underneath the Discovery. Now have a second look, being a little more thorough in case you missed something the first time – which, in all honesty, is very easy to do. Perhaps there were areas where you didn't look too closely, because you were concerned with the major problem area of the rear chassis.

Spread out a blanket or similar, and get under there to take a look. Better yet, if you're examining the vehicle in a garage, ask to put the vehicle on a hoist. Or, if the seller has an inspection pit, ask if the vehicle can be driven there so you can inspect it from underneath. Be warned: many pits collect water, and you may find yourself wading!

Steam in the exhaust is a bad sign. In this case, it indicated a leaking head gasket ...

... and this was the head gasket. The plastic dowels that locate the head had sheared, allowing the head to move slightly. The rusty marks show where the gasket had been leaking.

Oil and fluid leaks 4 3 2 1

If the Discovery is leaking oil or other fluids, the evidence will be obvious when you get underneath. Check where the leak is coming from. Engine oil is one obvious leak, and will typically be coming from the sump. However, if the leak is coming from the right-hand rear of the engine, accompanied by the smell of diesel, then it's probable that the fuel pressure regulator is faulty. This isn't very expensive but can be awkward to change, and an issue here makes a good bargaining point when negotiating a price for the vehicle.

Oil leaks may come from axle drain plugs that aren't sealed properly, but check for cracked differential or axle casings, especially on a Discovery that's been used a lot off-road. That sort of damage will be expensive to put right.

Note that major fluid leaks from the power steering system, either from

the hydraulic pipes or from the steering box, will lead to refusal of a roadworthiness certificate.

Have a second look at the rear chassis. It might have got worse since the first time you looked!

Chassis and suspension

   1

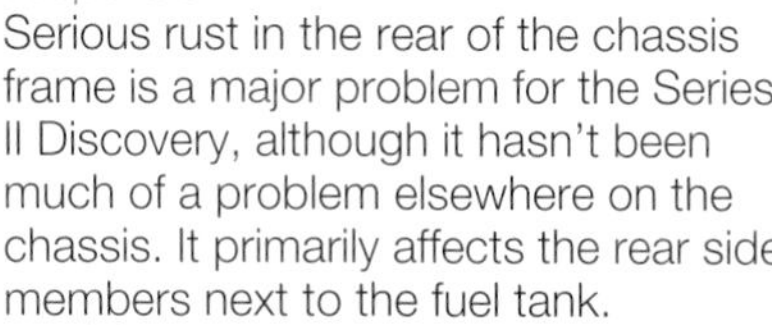

Serious rust in the rear of the chassis frame is a major problem for the Series II Discovery, although it hasn't been much of a problem elsewhere on the chassis. It primarily affects the rear side members next to the fuel tank.

You may have spotted rust in this area during your preliminary examination, and if you're still interested in the vehicle then it's likely to be for one of two reasons. One is that the rust doesn't yet look bad enough to cause concern – but bear in mind that rear chassis rust can go from an apparently minor problem to a fairly serious one in a matter of weeks, so don't be over-optimistic!

The second reason is that you believe the chassis is repairable. It may be, but simply plating over the rust is only going to delay the inevitable for a year or so. If you plan to deal with the job properly, there are several aftermarket part-chassis available. Remember, though, that these are major items that are expensive (although not unreasonably so) in themselves, and that fitting them is a major job that requires a lot of dismantling as well as a good deal of skill and patience.

It's advisable to understand how the vehicle's main systems work so that you can get an idea of what might be causing faults. This demonstration chassis, with Td5 engine, shows the pipes for the ACE system in red.

Realistically, the rest of the Discovery would have to be pretty good to justify the trouble and expense of a new rear chassis.

On those models with air suspension on the rear axle, there are some additional checks to make. First, check the base of each rubber air spring, where it meets the axle casing. These springs flex quite a lot in normal use, and eventually the rubber begins to split. With a little more wear, the split becomes an air leak.

Air springs can carry on for quite some time without giving any warning of a problem, because small leaks often seal themselves as the rubber settles differently. However, once a leak becomes more serious, it leads to problems. First – and very obviously – the vehicle may 'collapse' on the side where the spring is leaking, typically when left parked overnight. Normal height will be restored on start-up in the morning, so a vehicle can continue in use for some time in this condition. However, remember that the air springs are kept under pressure by the chassis-mounted air compressor, which only runs when the pressure drops below a set level. If the pressure drops regularly, the compressor will be triggered to run more frequently, and for longer periods, and eventually it will exceed its design limits and burn out. A replacement air compressor is expensive.

When checking a rear air suspension system, it is as well to check the condition of the height sensors, which are vertical rods (about as fat as a pencil) mounted to the axle casing at the bottom and to a plastic arm at the top that runs perpendicular to them. These are the triggers for the compressor; if the horizontal arm drops below a set level because the rear of the vehicle is sitting

This is one of the rams that operate the ACE system on the front axle. Normally, it wouldn't be painted red.

This is the valve block for the ACE system. All the pipes are specially shaped and must be replaced as a set, which makes them expensive.

low, the compressor is switched on and will pump up the springs. Obviously, any damage here will interfere with the correct working of the height-control system. Worth knowing is that an internal failure of the sensor can sometimes occur, and that there is no known way of predicting this!

Front and rear axles

The axle casings may show signs of off-road damage, typically around the differential housings because these hang lower than the rest of the casing. Severe damage is likely to lead to leaks from the differential, although these will be easy to spot.

At each end of the front axle is a chromed ball, which swivels to allow the wheels to be steered. The chromed faces should be smooth, not pitted or rusted. If sand or mud becomes trapped under the swivel seals, it will eventually scratch or erode the chrome surface so that the seal cannot work effectively, and at this point oil begins to leak out. Oil is essential to the workings of the steering here, and severe oil leaks indicate that the ball swivels (and maybe more) need to be replaced.

On the rear axle, check the security of the brake pipes that run along its casing. They will probably be held in place by plastic ties, but that's good enough to keep them out of harm's way.

The Series II Discovery has long-travel suspension to give a compliant ride, and cornering roll is tamed by anti-roll bars on the front and rear axles of all models. Some models have an ACE (Active Cornering Enhancement) roll control system as well. Check for worn rubber mounting bushes on the anti-roll bars by grasping each bar firmly and trying to move it back and forth. There are also several rubber bushes on the locating arms for both front and rear axles, and there should be no discernible play in these. In any case, worn bushes will become apparent during a test drive, when the vehicle will feel woolly, and may wander on the road.

When the ACE roll control system is fitted, the anti-roll bars are attached to hydraulic rams: there are two of these on the front bar and one on the rear bar. ACE works by using accelerometers mounted at strategic points in the body. When one of these detects the body beginning to lean, it sends a signal to the ACE control system, which in turn activates the rams, bringing the anti-roll bars into play and so limiting roll very effectively. Any problems with the ACE system, which is operated by fluid pressure, will be apparent on a test drive – even if the seller has disconnected the dashboard warning light.

Fuel tank, and LPG conversions

All Series II Discoverys have a plastic fuel tank which doesn't usually give trouble. However, it's wise to check the security of its fixings, and for any signs of impact damage to the steel protection plate underneath. This kind of damage can occur in off-road use.

The cost of running a V8-engined Discovery as an everyday vehicle has persuaded some owners to go for an LPG conversion. LPG fuel is subject to lower taxation than petrol and, although it's slightly less energy-efficient, it can therefore considerably reduce fuel costs.

An LPG conversion will normally include an extra fuel tank, often fitted under the right-hand side of the body behind the rear wheel. However, some less reputable converters took the easy way and fitted an extra tank in the load bay, where it obviously reduces load capacity. A Discovery converted to run on LPG normally

No problem here: the exhaust tail pipe of a diesel will typically be black inside, like this one. The reversing sensors visible in the bumper are actually aftermarket types, but are very similar to the Land Rover option.

retains the ability to run on petrol from the standard fuel tank as well. If an LPG system has been fitted, ask to see evidence that the system has been checked and approved as safe by an appropriate authority. Your insurer may well ask for an engineer's report, too.

Brakes

The Series II Discovery has disc brakes on all four wheels, the front pair being ventilated. The face-lift models from mid-2002 have discs of a different diameter from those on earlier models. These brakes give superb stopping power when in good order, the later system having noticeably more pedal feel than the early one. Check that the correct discs are fitted and that they aren't scored or rusty; rust works its way inwards from the outboard edge of a disc. Aftermarket cross-drilled discs have been made available and do a good job as replacements.

The handbrake operates on a drum directly behind the transfer gearbox. It locks movement of the rear propshaft, but of course can't compensate for any movement in the propshaft's universal joints. This accounts for the slight lurch that often occurs on a slope before the handbrake engages – a feature which many people find worrying. It's not unknown for the transmission brake itself to be damaged by a severe impact in off-road driving, but this sort of damage will be obvious.

Steering

Power-assisted steering was standard on all Series II Discovery models. Leaks do occur, and you'll have checked for obvious ones when looking underneath the vehicle. Bear in mind that the PAS fluid used in these vehicles is not the familiar red fluid used in many other vehicles. Land Rover always recommended a special cold-climate type which is a clear fluid; needless to say, it's far more expensive than ordinary PAS fluid!

The system shouldn't moan or hiss, although it may make protesting noises if the wheels are turned on a hard surface while the vehicle is stationary (as often happens in parking manoeuvres). If it does so in other circumstances, there's a problem.

To test for steering problems, you need to have an assistant. Ask them to turn the steering wheel from lock to lock while you get under the vehicle and check for fluid leaks from the PAS box, and for movement in the steering linkages. There should be no movement at all between the swivel pin housing and the swivel steering lever at the point where they're bolted together. Free movement in any of the steering assembly's ball joints points to wear.

There is of course also a steering damper, which runs horizontally ahead of the front axle. If there are problems here, your road test later will reveal excessive vibration through the steering wheel.

Dampers

It's difficult to test the dampers (shock absorbers) on a Discovery by the sort of bounce test that people commonly use for cars. So unless there are obvious fluid leaks from the dampers, or damage to their casings, wait until you drive the vehicle to assess their condition.

Propshafts

Check for wear in the transmission by grasping the front and rear propshafts in turn and trying to twist them. They will turn slightly as slack in the system is taken up, but if either will rotate as much as a quarter of a turn, there's excessive wear. This may well be in the appropriate differential. When testing the rear propshaft, make sure that the handbrake is off in order to get a true impression.

While looking at the transmission, check for wear in the universal joints on the propshaft ends by using a screwdriver as a lever to see if there is appreciable movement between the yoke and the joint. The more movement there is, the more advanced the wear will be. All Series II Discoverys have a rubber 'doughnut' joint where the rear propshaft meets the rear differential, to damp out transmission shocks and noise. You checked this during your initial evaluation, but have another good look now.

Exhaust system

The standard exhaust systems on the Series II Discovery are quite long-lived, especially those on the diesel models. A stainless steel system is a bonus, as it means you are unlikely ever to need a new exhaust. However, do ask to see evidence, such as an invoice, that the system really is stainless steel. It's also as well to check all the mountings, both rigid and flexible.

All petrol-engined Discoverys have (or should have) catalytic converters in the exhaust system. These 'cats' are very expensive to replace and owners often try to avoid the job, so it's worth checking that the 'cats' (one in the middle of each exhaust downpipe, at the back of the engine) are present. If the 'cat' rattles at idle when the engine is warm, it probably needs replacing. Needless to say, a vehicle originally fitted with a catalytic converter exhaust is required to have one to meet roadworthiness regulations in most countries.

There have been several aftermarket suppliers of 'sports' exhausts for the Series II Discovery. Typically, these systems dispense with the centre silencer, reducing the back pressure and allowing the engine to breathe more freely; an inevitable result (and one that attracts many buyers) is that the exhaust sounds louder and more sporty. There is no particular problem with such exhaust systems, as long as you are happy with the higher level of noise.

While examining the exhaust, it's worth checking the state of the tailpipe, too. On diesel models, the inside of the exhaust pipe is always likely to be a black colour. On petrol models, a light grey deposit inside the pipe is a good sign, but a powdery black deposit suggests the engine is running rich or that the vehicle has been used

There are multiple switches to check. These are on the front of the cubby box between the seats on an ES model, and control the electric windows and seat heaters.

The face panel of the ICE head unit on more expensive models is shaped to fit the facia. Also visible here is the control panel for the automatic climate control system: make sure it all works if you can.

excessively in low-speed town traffic.

When the engine is running, steam from the exhaust of either a petrol or diesel engine suggests head gasket problems (although there may be a small amount on starting a cold engine, caused by condensation in the exhaust pipe). White smoke may point to a leak from the brake servo.

Electrical system    1

The Series II Discovery generally has a much more robust electrical system than that on earlier Land Rover models. The system uses shaped plastic block connectors, which are fine when in good condition but a nightmare if they break or distort in old age. Although it's a good idea to check and clean connections (after purchase, obviously!), with these it's probably best to leave them well alone unless there's a problem.

The best general advice is to just make sure that everything electrical works. Lights are a bare minimum for legal and safety reasons, but check the electric windows and sunroofs if fitted, the central locking, the electric seat adjustment and seat heaters if fitted, and even the ICE system. The more expensive ICE head units in the Series II were tailored to fit the vehicle, although lower-specification models had standard DIN-sized head units. A radio that doesn't work shouldn't put you off buying a vehicle, but it's a bargaining point when you're trying to agree a price with the seller.

Lastly, take a long, careful look at any wiring that's not original to the vehicle, such as the power supply to a CB radio (whether or not the radio itself is still in place).

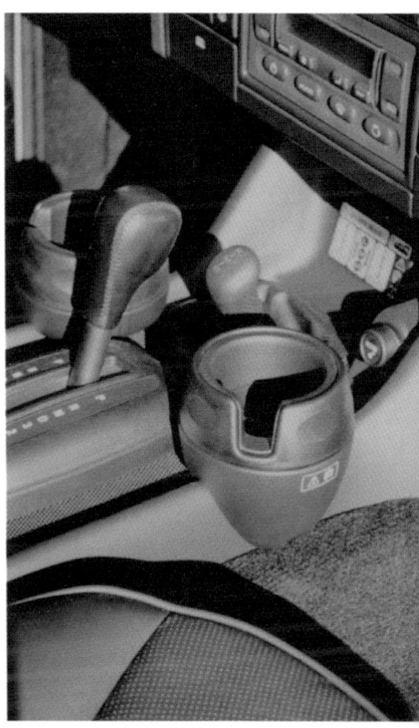

Front cupholders are usually in a sprung 'drawer' below the heating and ventilating controls, but these larger ones were introduced for US models, and became available as an accessory as well.

It's not unknown for additional equipment to overload the original wiring and burn it out.

Test drive

You will want to take the vehicle for a test drive before making the decision to buy. Double-check the position on insurance and that the vehicle remains road legal; both insurance and roadworthiness certificate may have expired since you took your earlier look!

Engine health and performance

Most people assume the health of the engine is the first thing to check on a test drive, so we'll start with that. But remember, it isn't always the engine that causes the most expensive problems!

• **The Td5 diesel**

The Td5 should pull strongly through the gears, and shouldn't feel sluggish at low speeds. This is a 'drive-by-wire' system, much mistrusted by Luddites when the Series II was new, although in practice it has always worked very well. There are two separate throttle maps in the ECU, which give a more gradual response to pressure on the accelerator when low range is selected (to give better control for difficult terrain) and a faster response in high range (for better on-road acceleration). If you notice a difference in response between the two modes, this is why. Note, too, that the Td5 engine for automatic models had more torque after mid-2002.

Keep an eye on the engine temperature gauge. If the temperature rises past a certain level, the 'limp home' mode will be activated automatically and only limited

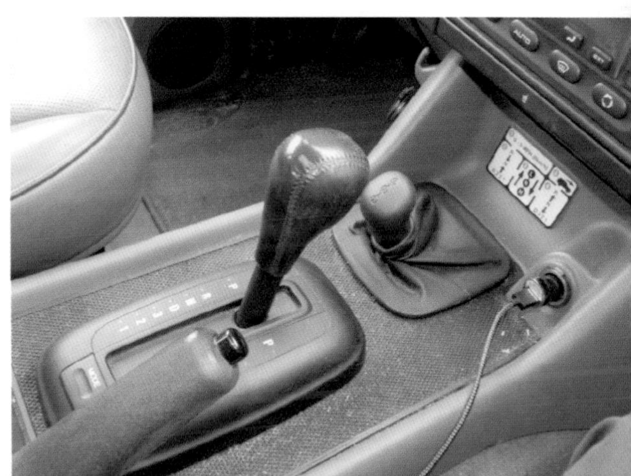

Check that the transmission controls all work correctly. In high range, the 'mode' switch at the back of the automatic selector delivers a more sporty shift pattern – although it makes little real difference to acceleration.

acceleration will be available. Overheating is fairly uncommon on these engines unless there is a coolant leak, but it's a known problem that the plastic dowels locating the cylinder head can crack after high mileages, allowing the head to move slightly and the cooling system to leak. You can't always detect this problem from a test drive, but if there's a strong smell of hot coolant, try to discover where it's coming from.

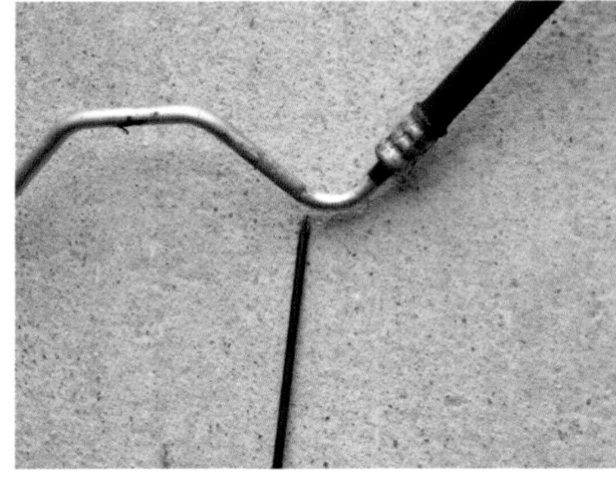

The screwdriver points to a tiny hole in one of the air conditioning pipes, which caused complete loss of refrigerant. This kind of damage is impossible to see during an inspection, so make sure the air conditioning works by running it.

When you return from your test drive, allow the warm engine to idle for a few seconds – which is good practice anyway, because it allows the turbocharger to slow down while its oil is still circulating. Then blip the accelerator and check in the mirror for black smoke from the exhaust. If there is some, the engine is worn.

• **The petrol V8**

One of the great attractions of the petrol V8 engine is its smooth and refined power delivery, and any engine that falls short of the mark should be treated with suspicion. Listen for top-end noise (the hydraulic tappets can gum up, and the camshaft can wear) and beware of misfires, which aren't always easy to detect in a multi-cylinder engine. A rough and rasping sound from one side of the engine usually means that the exhaust manifold is blowing; it's unlikely to be cracked, and the remedy should be nothing more expensive than tightening the manifold bolts.

Gearbox assessment

Series II Discoverys are available with manual or automatic gearboxes. The things to look out for will differ depending on the specification of the vehicle you are viewing. Use the check boxes that match the gearbox present.

• **Manual gearbox** 4 3 2 1

The manual gearbox is the five-speed R380 type (R for Rover Group, 380 for its torque capacity in Nm). Although early examples in earlier vehicles had some problems, these had been sorted out by the time of the Series II Discovery and the gearbox is generally not an issue. Gear selection should be smooth and baulk-free. However, high-mileage gearboxes do show signs of wear. With the engine running and the selector in neutral, listen for the rattle that indicates a worn layshaft.

The R380 can suffer from mainshaft wear and synchromesh problems, and sometimes no gear can be engaged until the gearbox has warmed up. Third gear seems to be most affected, so listen for a crunch as it's selected and as you change down to second. This gearbox was deliberately designed to give slick changes like those in a conventional car, and something is wrong if it doesn't.

Nevertheless, an R380 gearbox is quite capable of functioning for a very long time despite problems caused by wear. Be gentle with a worn one, and aim to fix it or replace it later. You can use demonstrable wear as a bargaining point.

If the clutch squeals when you push the pedal to the floor, the release bearing is probably worn. The parts aren't expensive but fitting can be costly unless you do it yourself, in which case it'll take quite a long time. If vehicle speed doesn't increase when you press the accelerator, the clutch is worn and is slipping. Expect the clutch to bite when the pedal is about half-way through its travel; near the top or near the bottom means the adjustment isn't right. Finally, if there's clutch judder as the drive is taken up, you'll need to take a closer look. Harsh gear changes that aren't down to a gearbox fault may be caused by a worn clutch fork.

• **Automatic gearbox** 4 3 2 1

The ZF four-speed automatic gearboxes are very robust and reliable. Changes are normally not very noticeable, so look out for any hesitation or slurring as the box changes up; it probably means the internal clutches are worn.

Transfer gearbox and differential lock 4 3 2 1

You checked that low ratio engages and that the differential lock (when fitted) works properly during your preliminary evaluation. Check them both again, just to be sure.

Steering 4 3 2 1

The steering on a Series II Discovery is generally well-weighted and well-suited to the vehicle. If you find that the vehicle you're testing suffers from wander, the problem is probably worn track rod ends or suspension bushes. If there seems to be rear-end steering in corners, the rear radius arm bushes are probably worn; check by accelerating and then lifting off in a corner.

When turning the steering on a stationary vehicle, you are putting a great strain on the power assistance system, so a few groans and creaks shouldn't be a cause for concern. However, if the steering makes similar noises on the move at low speeds, there's a serious problem.

Brakes, HDC and traction control 4 3 2 1

All Series II Discovery models have servo-assisted brakes with ABS, which should pull the vehicle up quickly and in a straight line. The brakes on the face-lift models built from mid-2002 will feel sharper than those on earlier models, but there seems to be no difference in their stopping ability. Land Rover aficionados will already know this, but to anyone new to the marque, do *not* test the handbrake by applying it when the vehicle is moving. The handbrake operates on the transmission, not the wheels, and applying it on the move may cause some expensive damage.

The ABS system makes some curious moaning noises as it cycles and recharges every few minutes, but you won't normally hear these unless the vehicle is stationary with the engine running. ABS will react to any loss of grip under braking by pumping the brakes rapidly and making a chattering noise which can be alarming until you recognise what it is.

Land Rover used the ABS system to operate two other driver aids on the Series II Discovery. One of these is ETC (Electronic Traction Control), which uses the wheel sensors to detect wheel slip and will pulse the brake on the affected wheel until traction is regained. This pulsing is accompanied by the same chattering noise that the ABS makes. One way of testing the ETC system, and of provoking that noise, is to put one wheel on a kerb and then pull away while steering onto the road; the momentary loss of traction as the wheel leaves the kerb and before it hits the road will usually be enough to trigger the system.

The second driver aid dependent on the ABS system is HDC (Hill Descent Control). This only works when low range is engaged, and is activated by a switch on the dashboard. It pulses the brakes to keep speed below a pre-set limit on steep downhill descents, preventing the vehicle from running away dangerously.

Unsurprisingly, when something goes wrong with one of these three interconnected systems, warning lights are triggered on the instrument panel. In the worst case, all three come on together, and they're known in Land Rover circles as the Three Amigos. If this happens, the problem usually lies with the ABS shuttle valve or with a wheel sensor; in either case, the fault needs to be dealt with immediately. If the Three Amigos come on during your test drive, use it as a bargaining counter to haggle the price down – or choose to buy another vehicle.

Paperwork

You looked at the paperwork when you did your preliminary assessment. Now's the time to double-check that everything really is in order.

Evaluation procedure

Add up the total points, and see what category the vehicle falls into. The maximum possible score is 100.

85 points = Excellent; 70 points = Good; 55 points = Average; 40 points = Poor.

A Discovery scoring over 70 will be completely usable and will need only regular care and maintenance to preserve its condition. A score between 50 and 60 means some work is needed, and this is likely to cost about the same regardless of the actual score. A score lower than 50 means that you are looking at some major restoration work, in which case it may be preferable to buy a better vehicle.

10 Auctions

– sold! Another way to buy your dream

Auction pros & cons

Pros: Prices will usually be lower than those of dealers or private sellers and you might grab a real bargain on the day. Auctioneers have usually established clear title with the seller. At the venue you can usually examine documentation relating to the vehicle.

Cons: You have to rely on a sketchy catalogue description of condition & history. The opportunity to inspect is limited and you can't drive the car. Auction cars are often a little below par and may require some work. It's easy to overbid. There will usually be a buyer's premium to pay in addition to the auction hammer price.

Which auction?

Auctions by established auctioneers are advertised in car magazines and on the auction houses' websites. A catalogue, or a simple printed list of the lots for auctions, might only be available a day or two ahead, though often lots are listed and pictured on auctioneers' websites much earlier. Contact the auction company to ask if previous auction selling prices are available as this is useful information (details of past sales are often available on websites).

Catalogue, entry fee and payment details

When you purchase the catalogue of the vehicles in the auction, it often acts as a ticket allowing two people to attend the viewing days and the auction. Catalogue details tend to be comparatively brief, but will include information such as 'one owner from new, low mileage, full service history,' etc. It will also usually show a guide price to give you some idea of what to expect to pay and will tell you what is charged as a 'buyer's premium.' The catalogue will also contain details of acceptable forms of payment. At the fall of the hammer an immediate deposit is usually required, the balance payable within 24 hours. If the plan is to pay by cash there may be a cash limit. Some auctions will accept payment by debit card. Sometimes credit or charge cards are acceptable, but will often incur an extra charge. A bank draft or bank transfer will have to be arranged in advance with your own bank as well as with the auction house. No vehicle will be released before **all** payments are cleared. If delays occur in payment transfers then storage costs can accrue.

Buyer's premium

A buyer's premium will be added to the hammer price: **don't** forget this in your calculations. It's not usual for there to be a further state tax or local tax on the purchase price and/or on the buyer's premium.

Viewing

In some instances it's possible to view on the day, or days before, as well as in the hours prior to, the auction. There are auction officials available who are willing to help out by opening engine and luggage compartments and to allow you to inspect the interior. While the officials may start the engine for you, a test drive is out of the question. Crawling under and around the car as much as you want is permitted, but you can't suggest that the car you are interested in be jacked up, or attempt to do the job yourself. You can also ask to see any documentation available.

Bidding

Before you take part in the auction, **decide your maximum bid – and stick to it!**

It may take a while for the auctioneer to reach the lot you are interested in, so use that time to observe how other bidders behave. When it's the turn of your car, attract the auctioneer's attention and make an early bid. The auctioneer will then look to you for a reaction every time another bid is made; usually the bids will be in fixed increments until the bidding slows, when smaller increments will often be accepted before the hammer falls. If you want to withdraw from the bidding, make sure the auctioneer understands your intentions – a vigorous shake of the head when he or she looks to you for the next bid should do the trick!

Assuming that you're the successful bidder, the auctioneer will note your card or paddle number, and from that moment on you will be responsible for the vehicle.

If the vehicle is unsold, either because it failed to reach the reserve or because there was little interest, it may be possible to negotiate with the owner, via the auctioneers, after the sale is over.

Successful bid

There are two more items to think about. How to get the Discovery home, and insurance. If you can't drive the vehicle, your own or a hired trailer is one way; another is to have the vehicle shipped using the facilities of a local company. The auction house will also have details of companies specialising in the transfer of cars.

Insurance for immediate cover can usually be purchased on site, but it may be more cost-effective to make arrangements with your own insurance company in advance, and then call to confirm the full details.

eBay & other online auctions?

eBay & other online auctions could land you a Discovery at a bargain price, though you'd be foolhardy to bid without examining it first, something most vendors encourage. A useful feature of eBay is that the geographical location of the vehicle is shown, so you can narrow your choices to those within a realistic radius of home. Be prepared to be outbid in the last few moments of the auction. Remember, your bid is binding and that it will be very, very difficult to get restitution in the case of a crooked vendor fleecing you – *caveat emptor!*

Be aware that some vehicles offered for sale in online auctions are 'ghost' cars. **Don't** part with **any** cash without being sure that the vehicle does actually exist and is as described (usually pre-bidding inspection is possible).

Auctioneers

Barrett-Jackson www.barrett-jackson.com
Bonhams www.bonhams.com
British Car Auctions (BCA) www.bca-europe.com or www.british-car-auctions.co.uk
Cheffins www.cheffins.co.uk
Christies www.christies.com
Coys www.coys.co.uk
eBay www.eBay.com
H&H www.classic-auctions.co.uk
RM www.rmsothebys.com
Shannons www.shannons.com.au
Silver www.silverauctions.com

11 Paperwork

– correct documentation is essential!

The paper trail

Classic, collector and prestige cars often come with a large portfolio of paperwork accumulated and passed on by a succession of proud owners. This documentation represents the real history of the car; from it you can deduce the level of care the car has received, how much it's been used, which specialists have worked on it and the dates of major repairs/restorations. All this information will be priceless to you as the new owner, so be wary of cars with little paperwork to support their claimed history.

Registration documents

All countries/states have some form of registration for private vehicles whether it's like the American 'pink slip' system or the British 'log book' system.

It's essential to check that the registration document is genuine, that it relates to the car in question, and that all the vehicle's details are correctly recorded, including chassis/VIN and engine numbers (if these are shown). If you're buying from the previous owner, their name and address will be recorded in the document: this won't be the case if you're buying from a dealer.

In the UK the current registration document, the 'V5C', has coloured sections of blue, green and pink. The blue section refers to the car specification, the green section has details of the new owner and the pink section is sent to the DVLA when the car is sold. A small yellow section deals with selling the car in the motor trade.

If the car has a foreign registration there may be expensive and time-consuming formalities to complete. Do you really want the hassle?

Previous ownership records

Due to important new legislation on data protection, it's no longer possible to acquire, from the British DVLA, a list of previous owners of a car you own, or are intending to purchase. This also applies to dealerships and other specialists, who you may wish to contact for information on previous ownership and repair work.

Roadworthiness certificate

Most country/state administrations require vehicles to be regularly tested to prove that they're safe to use on public highways and don't produce excessive emissions. In the UK the test (the 'MoT') is carried out at approved testing stations. In the USA the requirement varies, but most states insist on an emissions test every two years, minimum, while the police are charged with pulling over unsafe-looking vehicles.

The MoT is required yearly, once a vehicle becomes three years old. Of particular relevance for older cars is that the certificate issued includes the mileage reading recorded at the test and so becomes an independent record of the car's history. Ask if previous certificates are available. Without an MoT the vehicle should be trailered to its new home, unless you insist that a valid MoT is included. (Not such a bad idea, as at least you will know the car was roadworthy on the day it was tested.)

Road licence

Every country/state administration charges some kind of tax for the use of its roads, the actual form of the 'road licence' and how it's displayed varying enormously country to country and state to state.

Whatever the form of the 'road licence,' it must relate to the vehicle carrying it and must be present and valid if the car is to be driven legally on public highways.

New legislation in the UK means that the seller of a car must surrender any existing 'road licence,' and it's the responsibility of the new owner to re-tax the vehicle at the time of purchase, before the car can be driven on the road. It's therefore vital to see the Vehicle Registration Certificate (V5C) at the time of purchase, and to have access to the New Keeper Supplement (V5C/2), allowing the buyer to obtain road tax immediately.

In the UK if a car is untaxed due to not being used for some time, the owner must inform the licencing authorities, or the vehicle's date-related registration number will be lost and there'll be a painful amount of paperwork to get it re-registered.

Certificates of authenticity

For many collectible cars it's possible to get a certificate proving the age and authenticity (engine and chassis numbers, paint colour, trim) of a particular vehicle; sometimes called 'Heritage Certificates,' it's a definite bonus if the car comes with one. If you want to get one, the relevant owners' club is the best starting point.

Valuation certificate

Hopefully, the vendor will have a recent valuation certificate, or letter signed by a recognised expert stating how much he, or she, believes the particular car to be worth (such documents, together with photos, are usually needed to get 'agreed value' insurance). Generally such documents should act only as confirmation of your own assessment of the car rather than a guarantee of value as the expert has probably not seen the car in the flesh. The easiest way to find out how to obtain a formal valuation is to contact the owners' club.

Service history

Often these cars will have been serviced at home by enthusiastic (hopefully capable) owners for a good number of years. Nevertheless, try to obtain as much service history and other paperwork pertaining to the car as you can. Naturally, dealer stamps, or specialist garage receipts score most points in the value stakes. However, anything helps in the great authenticity game. Items like the original bill of sale, handbook, parts invoices and repair bills add to the story and character of the car. Even a brochure correct to the year of the car's manufacture is a useful document and something that could be hard to find in the future. In the case of a restoration, expect receipts and other evidence from a specialist restorer.

If the seller claims to have carried out regular servicing, ask what work was completed, when, and seek some evidence of it being carried out. Your assessment of the car's overall condition should tell you whether the seller's claims are genuine.

Restoration photographs

If the seller says that the vehicle has been restored, expect to see a series of photographs showing the restoration. Pictures taken at various stages, from various angles, should help you gauge the thoroughness of the work. If you buy the car, ask to take the photographs; they form an important part of the vehicle's history. It's surprising how many sellers are happy to part with their car and accept your cash, but want to keep their photographs! You may be able to persuade them to make copies.

12 What's it worth?

– let your head rule your heart

Condition

If the Discovery you've been looking at is really bad, then you've probably not bothered to use the marking system in chapter 9. You may not have even got as far as using that chapter at all!

If you did use the marking system in chapter 9 you'll know whether the Discovery is in Excellent (maybe Concours), Good, Average or Poor condition or, perhaps, somewhere in-between these categories.

Many specialist magazines run a regular price guide. If you haven't bought the latest editions, do so now to compare their suggested values for the model you're interested in: look at the auction prices they're reporting too. Series II Discovery values were low at the time of writing, but some models are always more in demand than others. Trends can change too.

The values published in the magazines tend to vary from one magazine to another, as do their scales of condition, so read the guidance notes they provide. Bear in mind that a really top-class, low-mileage Series II Discovery could be worth more than the highest scale published. Assuming that the one you have in mind is not top-class, relate the level of condition that you judge it to be in with the appropriate guide price. How does the figure compare with the asking price?

Before you start haggling with the seller, consider what effect any variation from standard specification might have on the car's value. If you are buying from a dealer, remember there will be a dealer's premium on the price.

The face-lift cars had different rear lights as well as different headlights. Is this important to you?

This 2001 Td5 model has one of the less comprehensive specifications, with an unpainted front apron and no auxiliary driving lights. But it would still be an excellent buy.

One of the smarter wheel styles is seen here on a US-model Series II Discovery. Wheels can make a big difference to the appearance of a vehicle ... but they can always be changed.

Desirable options/extras

Many owners consider the most desirable vehicles to be the better-equipped ones with features like automatic climate control, automatic gearbox, self-levelling rear suspension, and so on. These features certainly make it easier to live with a Series II Discovery. Extras are much more a matter of personal preference. For example, side steps may not improve the appearance of the vehicle but they may be necessary to help some people get in, as it sits quite high off the ground. It's worth knowing that the side steps offered by Land Rover look much better than many aftermarket types.

The base-model steel wheels were actually very rare in the UK, although more common on export models.

The rear air-conditioning system was a rare option, but is it worth paying extra to get it?

Undesirable features

What is desirable and what is undesirable in a Series II Discovery is governed by what you intend to do with the vehicle. If you are buying it for some off-road fun, then suspension lifts, chequer plate, a winch and some performance add-ons may be just what you are looking for.

Generally speaking, though, non-original features will detract from a vehicle's value – and maybe from its interest as well, if you're looking for a Discovery that's truly representative of the way they were. In that case, avoid those that have been extensively modified, or at least those which have been modified so much that they can't realistically be put back to original condition.

Whether you want aftermarket accessories that were contemporary with the vehicle is a matter of personal choice. Arguably, they were part of the way it was when new or nearly new. Another argument is that they were not fitted by the factory or one of its dealers and are therefore not 'original.'

Ask yourself whether the level of trim and equipment really matters to you. This LE trim was for the US market.

Striking a deal

Negotiate on the basis of your condition assessment, mileage, and fault rectification cost. Also take into account the car's specification. Be realistic about the value, but don't be completely intractable: a small compromise on the part of the vendor or buyer will often facilitate a deal at little real cost.

Some people are fascinated by special editions; others can take them or leave them.

13. Do you really want to restore?

– it'll take longer and cost more than you think

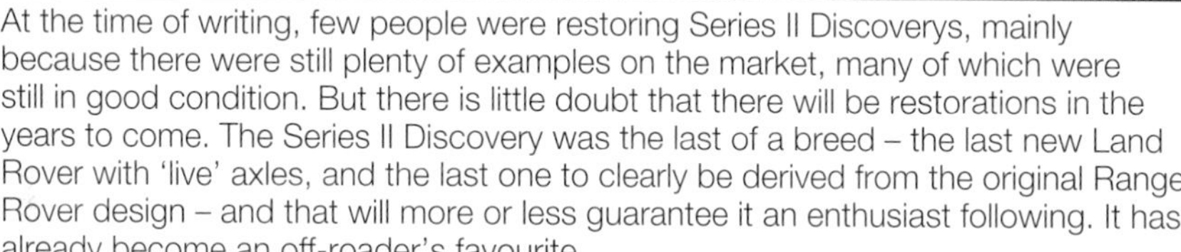

At the time of writing, few people were restoring Series II Discoverys, mainly because there were still plenty of examples on the market, many of which were still in good condition. But there is little doubt that there will be restorations in the years to come. The Series II Discovery was the last of a breed – the last new Land Rover with 'live' axles, and the last one to clearly be derived from the original Range Rover design – and that will more or less guarantee it an enthusiast following. It has already become an off-roader's favourite.

However, you may have found one that is particularly interesting, which you believe deserves a full restoration. Perhaps it was owned by a relative, and has some special meaning to you? Perhaps it's a rare special edition, and you appreciate its differences from the run-of-the-mill models? Perhaps you just like it, and want to restore it to its former glory – an expression which has become a cliché among car enthusiasts and usually implies spending a lot of money!

If you're dead set on restoring a vehicle, you need to know what to expect once the panels come off. This is a Series II Discovery bodyshell on the assembly lines at the Land Rover factory.

Whatever the reason, be realistic about what you are able to achieve. Easiest of all is a rolling restoration, which means that the vehicle remains useable for most of the time, and you improve it in larger or smaller bites as you go along. Hardest of all is the complete restoration of a derelict vehicle.

Cost will play a very big part in what you do. It has long been a maxim in the classic vehicle world that any restoration will take twice as long and cost at least twice as much as your original, hard-headed estimate. And forget the idea that you'll be able to sell the completed vehicle for more than you have spent on

You should have a clear idea of the vehicle's mechanical layout, too. This 'ghosted' drawing was produced when the model was new.

The roof-mounted video screen was rare, too. Here it is in use ...

It's always tempting to add extras that your vehicle never had when new! This is a sunglasses holder, mounted above the driver's door. It's very handy, but also rare.

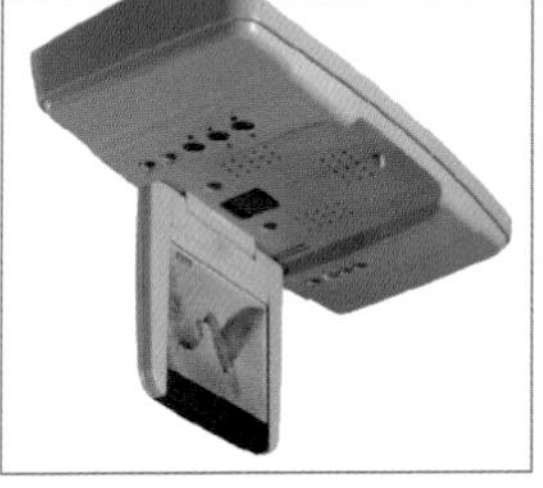

... and this is what it looks like out of the car.

it. Prices might rise that much in the next few years, but there's also a good chance that they won't.

So if you decide to restore a Series II Discovery, restore it for yourself. Restore it to your standards, to your time-scale, and to your budget. Even if you have the skills, the equipment and the premises to do the job, resign yourself to having no free weekends for at least a couple of years. If you don't have all these vital elements and are paying somebody else to do the work, resign yourself to having no money to spend on anything else for a similar period of time: Land Rover specialists and restorers can and do charge handsomely for deploying their skills. And whichever way you decide to go, resign yourself to frustrating waits while vital parts are sourced – or, in a worst case, re-made from scratch.

But don't let all this put you off. It's just a look on the bleak side to provoke you into thinking hard about what you're getting into. If you really are committed to getting that Discovery up and running and looking the way you think it should, the time, the effort and the money will all be worth it in the end. And after that, every little improvement you make will make you feel prouder and prouder. It may well become a long-term commitment, but you'll almost certainly find that it's worth it.

14 Paint problems

– bad complexion, including dimples, pimples and bubbles

Paint faults generally occur due lack of protection/maintenance, or to poor preparation prior to a respray or touch-up. Some of the following conditions may be present in the car you're looking at:

Orange peel

This appears as an uneven paint surface, similar to the appearance of the skin of an orange. The fault is caused by the failure of atomized paint droplets to flow into each other when they hit the surface. It's sometimes possible to rub out the effect with proprietary paint cutting/rubbing compound or very fine grades of abrasive paper. A respray may be necessary in severe cases. Consult a bodywork repairer/paint shop for advice on the particular car.

Orange peel.

Cracking

Severe cases are likely to have been caused by too heavy an application of paint (or filler beneath the paint). Also, insufficient stirring of the paint before application can lead to the components being improperly mixed, and cracking can result. Incompatibility with the paint already on the panel can have a similar effect. To rectify the problem it is necessary to rub down to a smooth, sound finish before respraying the problem area.

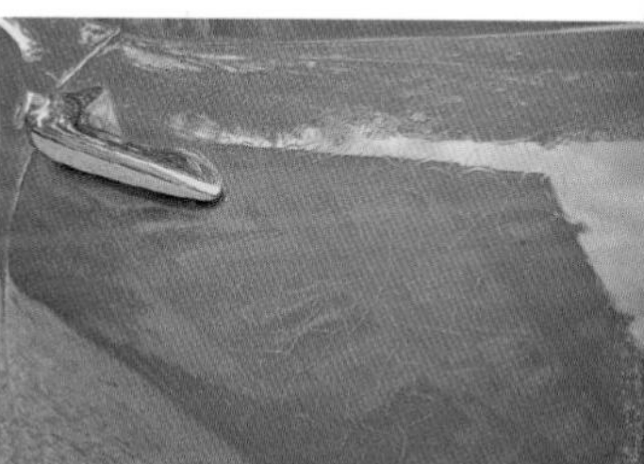

Cracking and crazing.

Crazing

Sometimes the paint takes on a crazed rather than a cracked appearance when the problems mentioned under 'Cracking' are present. This problem can also be caused by a reaction between the underlying surface and the paint. Paint removal and respraying the problem area is usually the only solution.

Micro blistering.

Blistering

This is almost always caused by corrosion of the metal beneath the paint. Usually perforation will be found in the metal and the damage will often be worse than that suggested by the area of blistering. The metal will have to be repaired before repainting.

Micro blistering

Usually the result of an economy respray where inadequate heating has allowed moisture to settle on the car before spraying. Consult a paint specialist, but usually damaged paint will have to be removed before partial or full respraying. Can also be caused by car covers that don't 'breathe.'

Fading

Some colours, especially reds, are prone to fading if subjected to strong sunlight for long periods without the benefit of polish protection. Sometimes proprietary paint restorers and/or paint cutting/rubbing compounds will retrieve the situation. Often a respray is the only real solution.

Peeling

Often a problem with metallic paintwork when the sealing laquer becomes damaged and begins to peel off. Poorly applied paint may also peel. The remedy is to strip and start again!

Dimples

Dimples in the paintwork are caused by the residue of polish (particularly silicone types) not being removed properly before respraying. Paint removal and repainting is the only solution.

Dents

Small dents are usually easily cured by the 'Dentmaster,' or equivalent process, that sucks or pushes out the dent (as long as the paint surface is still intact). Companies offering dent removal services usually come to your home: consult your telephone directory.

15 Problems due to lack of use

– just like their owners, Series II Discoverys need exercise!

Cars, like humans, are at their most efficient if they exercise regularly. A run of at least ten miles, once a week, is recommended for classics.

Seized components

Pistons in callipers, slave and master cylinders can seize. The clutch may seize if the plate becomes stuck to the flywheel, and pistons can seize in the bores, both due to corrosion. Handbrakes (parking brakes) can seize if the cables and linkages rust.

It's also worth knowing what type of use it had before it was laid up! The accessories and tyres may give it away, as they would on this one used for a long-distance expedition.

Fluids

Old, acidic oil can corrode bearings. Uninhibited coolant can corrode internal waterways – a particular problem with the V8 engine, which has aluminium heads and block. Lack of antifreeze can cause core plugs to be pushed out, even cracks in the block or head. Silt settling and solidifying can cause overheating. Brake fluid absorbs water from the atmosphere and should be renewed every two years. Old fluid with a high water content can cause corrosion and pistons/calipers to seize (freeze) and can cause brake failure when the water turns to vapour near hot braking components.

Much the same can be said for this one. Both vehicles have a 'snorkel' which prevents the engine from ingesting water when wading.

Tyre problems

Tyres on a car that has been stationary for some time will develop flat spots, resulting in some (usually temporary) vibration. If the tyre walls have cracks or (blister-type) bulges, new tyres are needed.

Shock absorbers (dampers)

With lack of use, the dampers will lose their elasticity or even seize. Creaking, groaning and stiff suspension are signs of this problem.

Rubber and plastic

Radiator hoses can perish and split, possibly resulting in the loss of all coolant. Window and door seals can harden and leak. Gaiters/boots can crack. Wiper blades will harden.

Electrics

The battery will be of little use if it hasn't been charged for many months. Earthing/grounding problems are common when the connections have corroded. The Discovery's electrics depend heavily on shaped plastic block connectors, and unless there's a specific problem, it's wise to leave these undisturbed. Sparkplug electrodes will often have corroded in an unused engine. Wiring insulation can harden and fail.

Rotting exhaust system

Exhaust gas contains a high water content, so exhaust systems corrode quickly from the inside when the vehicle is not used.

Air suspension

On models with air suspension, expect to replace the air springs as an absolute minimum. Height sensors, compressor and air reservoir may all need to be replaced as well before the system will work properly.

This unusual corporate colour scheme was on a Discovery owned by a construction company. It was probably used on muddy building sites, so you'd be wise to check the condition of the underside in this case.

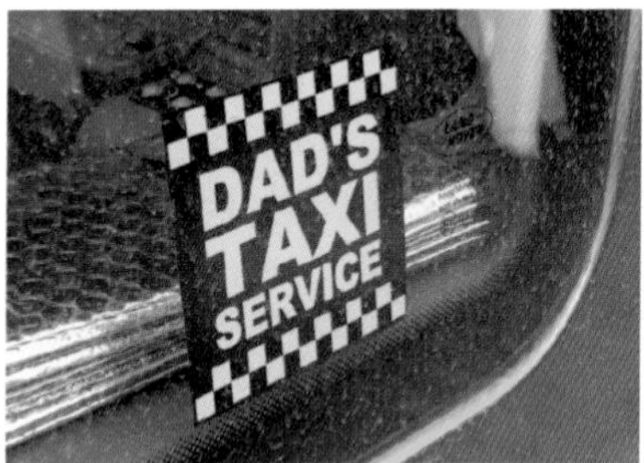

Realistically, most Discoverys will have had this sort of usage ...

16 The Community

– key people, organisations and companies in the Discovery world

The Discovery enjoys a special place in the hearts of Land Rover people world-wide. It may lack the luxury of a Range Rover (although the ES models run pretty close), but it's more family-friendly, and more suitable for everyday use than a utility Land Rover. Large numbers of enthusiasts find that it fits the bill perfectly, serving as weekday transport and weekend toy. As a result, there is plenty of specialist support available from parts suppliers and independent workshops.

The lists here are confined to the UK, but even then they're far from exhaustive. For details of clubs, specialists and suppliers in other countries, please consult your favourite 4x4 or Land Rover magazine, or check on the internet.

Clubs

There are many local and regional Land Rover clubs in the UK that welcome Series II Discoverys. However, you may find that the emphasis of your local club is more on off-road driving (typically greenlaning) or on competitive motorsport (typically trialling) than on meticulous restoration for what US enthusiasts call 'show 'n' shine' events. Many clubs of course cater for all forms of the hobby.

There is one club that is dedicated to Discoverys of all generations, and that is the Discovery Owners' Club. You can find it on the web at www.discoveryownersclub.org and if you're interested in joining, the Membership Secretary can be contacted by e-mail at memsec@discoveryownersclub.org.

There are multiple regional Land Rover clubs throughout North America, they can be found via your web browser.

Autojumbles and Land Rover shows may offer you a chance to find spare parts at very reasonable prices. But they won't often be in this sort of condition! These lenses were pictured when new, alongside the Discovery assembly lines.

Main spares suppliers

There are many suppliers of new spares for the Series II Discovery, and this list shows only the major ones in the UK. A web search will quickly find specialists in other countries:

- **John Craddock Ltd**, North Street, Bridgtown, Cannock, Staffordshire WS11 0AZ. 01543 577207, or www.johncraddockltd.co.uk
- **Paddock Spares and Accessories**, The Showground, The Cliff, Matlock, Derbyshire DE4 5EW. 01629 760877, www.paddockspares.com or sales@paddockspares.com
- **Rimmer Brothers**, Triumph House, Sleaford Road, Bracebridge Heath, Lincoln LN4 2NA. 01522 568000, www.rimmerbros.co.uk or LRsales@rimmerbros.co.uk

Specialist restorers

At the time of writing, Series II Discovery prices were generally low, with the result that few owners

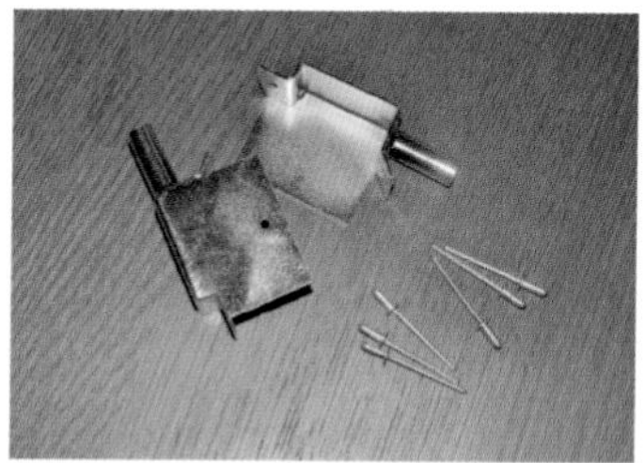

There are some useful aftermarket items to be found. These metal replacements for the notoriously fragile sunroof drain elbows are unlikely to break.

The Land Rover enthusiast community does like to adorn its vehicles with off-roading extras. Contrasting with its expensive-looking alloy wheels, this Discovery has a snorkel for wading, and that chequer-plate allows someone to stand on the bonnet without denting the panel underneath.

were prepared to spend large sums of money on restoration or refurbishment. As a result, there was a lack of specialist restorers in the trade, and many Discovery owners relied on replacement parts sourced from scrapyards.

However, any competent independent Land Rover workshop will probably be prepared to discuss major mechanical refurbishment of a Series II Discovery. Just be sure that you agree in advance exactly what you want to be done.

Off-road driving is not all about extreme challenges, as these Discoverys demonstrate.

Vehicle information

If you want to find out about the history of your own vehicle, start with the archives section of the British Motor Museum at Gaydon (01926 641188). They can normally tell you when your Series II Discovery left the factory en route for a Land Rover dealer (which will be a few days after it was actually built on the assembly lines), and who that dealer was. Their records will also reveal what colour it was originally. For a fee, they will provide you with a certificate that contains the available details and is a worthwhile addition to any enthusiast's vehicle paperwork.

Magazines

- **Land Rover Monthly**, The Publishing House, 2 Brickfields Business Park, Woolpit, Suffolk IP30 9QS. www.lrm.co.uk
- **Land Rover Owner International**, Bauer, Media House, Lynchwood, Peterborough PE2 6EA. www.lro.com

Books

- **How to modify Land Rover Discovery, Defender & Range Rover**, by Ralph Hosier. Veloce Publishing, ISBN 978-1-845843-15-1
- **Land Rover Discovery**, by Dave Pollard. Haynes Publishing, ISBN 978-1-844255-57-3
- **Land Rover Discovery 4x4 Performance Portfolio 1989-2000 (Brooklands Books Road Test Series)**, by RM Clarke. Brooklands Books Ltd, ISBN 1-855-20559-8
- **Land Rover Discovery. 25 Years of the Family 4x4**, by James Taylor. The Crowood Press Ltd, ISBN 978-1-84797-689-5
- **Land Rover Emergency Vehicles**, by James Taylor. Veloce Publishing, ISBN 978-1-787112-44-5
- **Land Rovers in British Military Service – Coil Sprung Models 1970-2007**, by James Taylor and Geoff Fletcher. Veloce Publishing, ISBN 978-1-787112-40-7

Modified? Just a little! Dave Thomas took this picture of an extensively modified Series II in Malta. The conversion has been excellently done.

17 Vital statistics

– essential data at your fingertips

Production history

It helps to understand what you're looking at if you have some idea of how the Series II Discovery evolved during six years in production. So here's a breakdown of the key changes; there were many more minor ones.

September 1998	Introduced, with 136bhp 2.5-litre Td5 diesel or 182bhp 4.0-litre V8 petrol engines; choice of manual or automatic gearboxes; five-seat and seven-seat configurations; S, GS, XS and ES trim levels.
Autumn 2000	E and Adventurer trim levels added; new Drystone cloth upholstery.
September 2001	Centre differential lock (which was never connected to a control) deleted from transfer box. Manual V8 models deleted for European markets.
June 2002	Face-lift, with new headlamps and tail lamps, new front spoiler, restyled alloy wheels, and interior changes. Manually controlled centre differential lock added. 217bhp 4.6-litre V8 replaced 4.0-litre type for North America.
September 2003	'3D' bonnet lettering; thicker 'Aero' roof bars on some models.
February 2004	Run-out Definitive Editions introduced: Pursuit, Landmark and ES Premium.
May 2004	Last Discovery Series II built.

You'll find the VIN in two separate places on a Series II Discovery. It's on this plate mounted to the bonnet lock platform ...

... and also on a small plate between dashboard and windscreen.

Chassis numbers

All Discovery Series II models had VIN-type chassis numbers consisting of 17 digits. The last six digits were the serial number and the first 11 contain information about the specification. They break down like this:

SAL*	Manufacturer code (Rover Group)
LT	Discovery Series II
G	Discovery Series II in standard specification
A	Discovery Series II for Japan
M	Standard body configuration
	Engine Specification
1	4.0-litre V8 for Australia
2	4.0-litre V8 for EEC and Japan
3	4.0-litre V8 for other countries
7	Td5 diesel for all countries except (8) and (9)
8	Td5 diesel for UK
9	Td5 diesel for Australia, EEC and Japan
	Steering and Gearbox Specification
3	RHD with 4-speed automatic gearbox
4	LHD with 4-speed automatic gearbox
7	RHD with 5-speed manual gearbox
8	LHD with 5-speed manual gearbox
	Model Year
X	1999
Y	2000
1	2001
2	2002
3	2003
4	2004
	Assembly
A	Assembled at Solihull
F	Shipped as KD for overseas assembly

The NAS (North American Specification) prefix codes differed, as follows:

SAL*	Manufacturer code (Rover Group)
	Trim and Seat Specification
TY	Discovery Series II with leather trim and five seats
TH	Adventurer LE, five seats
TJ	Adventurer LE, seven seats
TK	Duragrain trim, seven seats
TL	Duragrain trim, five seats
TM	Cloth trim, five seats
TN	Cloth trim, seven seats
TP	HSE with five seats, 2003 and later
TR	HSE with seven seats, 2003 and later
TW	Leather trim, seven seats
	Door Specification
1	Five-door body
	Engine Specification
3	4.0-litre V8
4	4.6-litre V8
	Gearbox Specification
4	4-speed automatic
	Security Check Digit
1 digit; either 0 to 9, or X	
	Model Year
X	1999
Y	2000
1	2001
2	2002
3	2003
4	2004
	Assembly
A	Assembled at Solihull

*These codes are present on every Discovery.

SpeedPro Series

How to modify

LAND ROVER

DISCOVERY, DEFENDER & RANGE ROVER

for high performance & serious off-road action

Ralph Hosier

Land Rover Discovery 1989 to 1998, Land Rover 90, 110 and Defender 1983 to 2010, Range Rover 1970 to 1995

Also includes information on servicing, repair, racing, expeditions and trekking, plus a buyers' guide

a Range Rover, Land Rover Discovery or Defender can be just the st
rful adventure. This book describes the options available to the owne
els and suspension lifts, under-body protection and tuning ideas, rig
convert the car into a high speed racer or an international expedition
clear, jargon-free instructions, advice on events like family weekend g
, international expeditions and full-on competition, accompanied by c
graphs throughout, this is the definitive guide to getting the most from
exciting vehicles.

ISBN: 978-1-845843-15-1
Paperback • 25x20.7cm • 128 pages • 312 colour pictures

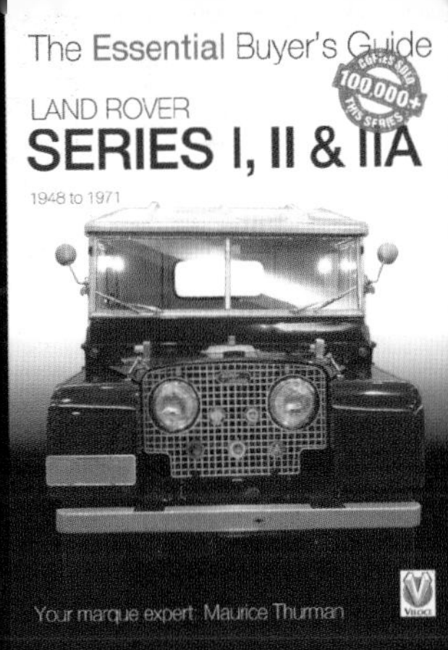

ISBN: 978-1-845850-14-2

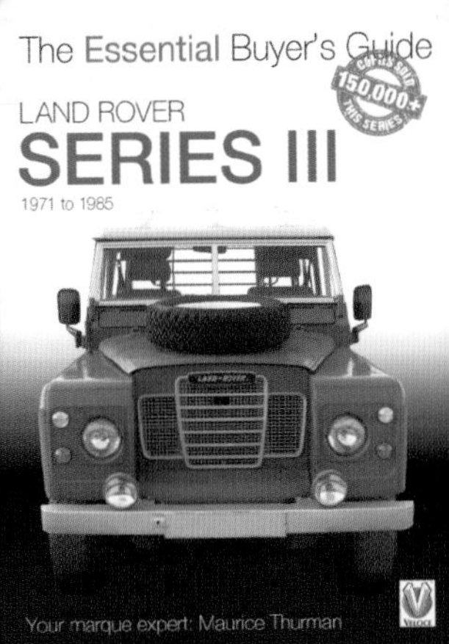

ISBN: 978-1-845844-42-4

ISBN: 978-1-787112-22-3

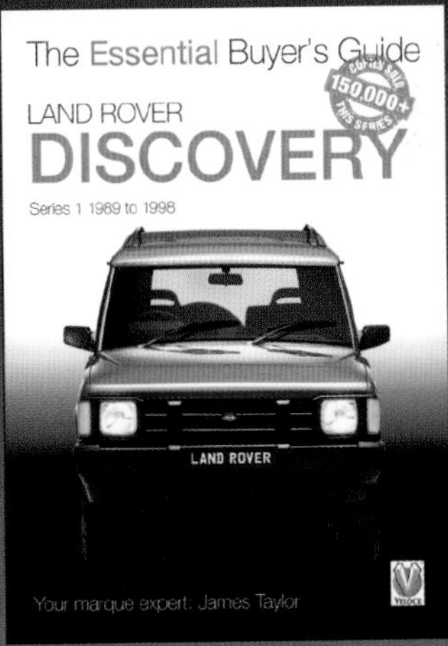

ISBN: 978-1-787113-00-8

Having these books in your pocket is just like having a real marque expert by your side. Benefit from the author's years of real ownership experience, learn how to spot a bad vehicle quickly, and how to assess a promising one like a professional. Get the right car at the right price!

For more information and price details, visit our website at www.veloce.co.uk
email: info@veloce.co.uk • Tel: +44(0)1305 260068

The Essential Buyer's Guide™ series ...

Index